The Comedy Bible

The complete resource for aspiring comedians

Brian McKim & Traci Skene

The Comedy Bible

The complete resource for aspiring comedians

Brian McKim & Traci Skene

A QUINTET BOOK

First edition for the United States and Canada
published in 2011 by Barron's Educational Series, Inc.

All inquiries should be addressed to:
Barron's Educational Series, Inc.
250 Wireless Boulevard
Hauppauge, NY 11788
www.barronseduc.com

Library of Congress Control Number: 2011920044

ISBN: 978-0-7641-6473-6

QTT.COMB

Conceived, designed, and produced by
Quintet Publishing Limited
The Old Brewery
6 Blundell Street
London N7 9BH
UK

Project Editors: Martha Burley, Ruth Patrick
Consultant: Rita Powers
Designer: Emma Wicks
Copy Editor: Nikky Twyman
Illustrator: Claire Scully
Art Editor: Zoë White
Art Director: Michael Charles
Managing Editor: Donna Gregory
Publisher: Mark Searle

Printed in China by 1010 Printing International Limited

9 8 7 6 5 4 3 2 1

TO OUR PARENTS, JOSEPH
DANIEL MCKIM & HELEN
CECILIA FEAN AND JAMES
DUNCAN SKENE & ROBERTA
EMMA DINGLER

CONTENTS

FOREWORD

It's quite a thrill to make someone laugh. Ask anyone who has ever done it. We've been doing it—on purpose, repeatedly, as standup comics—since the middle of the 1980s. We've performed in every imaginable kind of venue and appeared on network television—all because we have figured out a way to make people laugh.

Do you want to be a comedian? This book gives you permission to try. (Of course, you don't need our permission … but you knew that all along, didn't you?) Along with all the practical and useful tips, factoids, and suggestions, we have included oddball theories, wacky concepts, unforgettable quotes, and quirky bits of history designed to put this whole comedy thing in context.

The first six chapters explore the basics of writing and performing comedy. Chapter 7, entitled "Sketch writing," was written by *Saturday Night Live* sketch writer Ali Farahnakian. The chapter details his journey from college student, through Chicago's Second City, to his experience on the most celebrated comedy sketch show in the history of television. You'll also learn about premises, the evolution of sketch, sketch types … even how to end a sketch. Chapter 8 looks into writing sitcom scripts. Chapter 9 outlines writing for the printed word. In the last chapter, we talk about headshots, press kits, fan clubs, agents, managers—all those things you need to consider if you get really "serious" about being "funny."

After that, it's up to you decide when, where, and how you want to be part of it.

Brian McKim and Traci Skene

INTRODUCTION

The late, great comedian Mitch Hedberg famously said, "You can't please all of the people all of the time … and last night all those people were at my show." Hedberg, of course, was exaggerating. Or was he?

Good times, bad times

Standup comics, comedy writers, comedic actors, talk-show hosts, class clowns—and anybody else who has ever created or delivered a joke—know exactly what it feels like to displease an audience. They could be performing to just one person or to an audience of millions, but the feeling is no different. These performers also know just what it feels like to please an audience. This audience may be one critic, a comedy club audience, an editor, or even the cute temp worker at the next cubicle; but, again, the feeling remains exactly the same. The true comic is willing to endure the former scenario in order to experience the latter.

Hard knock life

There's a reason why people say comedy is hard. That's because it is! To be sure, the actual process of becoming a comedian presents many challenges, and anyone who says it's easy being a comedian or a comedy writer is lying. But there are no real impediments to *attempting* comedy. There

are no special schools or programs that one must enroll in to become a comedian; no guilds that one must join. Comedians aren't drawn from an exclusive class or societal stratum or a particular color or gender. Comics aren't required to be handsome, or pretty, or thin, or "classically trained." They're merely required to be funny.

IT'S A LOTTERY

There is a saying among comics: "They don't pay me for the shows that go great … they pay me for the ones that go horribly." In other words, when you're up there killing, and the crowd is gasping for air and the show is going about as good as it's ever gone, it isn't work, it's a pleasure. The flip side, however, is an encounter with a ghastly venue or a miserable crowd—or a combination of both—and then having to be up there on the stage is sheer drudgery. Some folks say they would do it all for free if every single show went really well. And those people will also tell you that no amount of money can soften the blow of a horrific experience. Of course, the truth lies somewhere in between the two.

U.K. comedians Eric Morecambe and Ernie Wise onstage during a comedy routine in December 1963.

The only thing tougher than comedy is a comedian.

Traci Skene

It looks easy ...

Does being funny guarantee success? No, but one thing is sure: if you aren't remotely funny, this means you are absolutely guaranteed to fail. And, whether you want to be a standup comic, or a sketch writer, or a radio personality, or a television presenter, or a comedic actress, there are lots of things that you need to learn and plenty of skills to acquire. Comedy may appear freewheeling and effortless, but such seeming ease is only achieved after a lot of experience and hard work—physical and mental. The goal, after all, for most (if not all) comedians is to make it look easy.

... but it isn't

However much easier the writing or performing of comedy may become, it never gets easy. There probably won't be a point when you say to yourself, "I am done. I have achieved it all. From now on, everything will fall neatly into place. I have crafted a formula with which I can easily create my comedy and it will, from this point forward, only be a matter of executing it and then standing back and watching the torrent of money, fame, riches, and laughter wash over me."

No barriers

The appeal of comedy is that it presents challenges at all points along the journey. And, fortunately, there's no age requirement for comedy, nor is there a retirement age. So, if you start young, you might look forward to a long and fulfilling career. If you start late, you won't be barred entry and you will be able to perfect your craft until well into your twilight years.

"I have seen what a laugh can do. It can transform almost unbearable tears into something bearable, even hopeful." Bob Hope (opposite).

"You go on in front of 10,000 people, you're supposed to be a little bit nervous. Excitement is what you should have." Bill Burr

1

SO ... YOU WANT TO BE A COMEDIAN

Even the best comedians find it hard to make an audience laugh on command, and this is why there's no such thing as a "proven comic." The only proven comic is the one who's getting laughs *right now*, and once they die down, he or she has to prove him- or herself all over again with the next joke. Such is the unforgiving nature of the comedy audience. Excellent comics realize the unrelenting nature of this challenge. They work extremely hard to appear as though they can make people laugh at will. That's to say, comedy never gets easy. It is sometimes likened to golf, in that Tiger Woods can birdie one hole, then wind up with a triple bogie. However, he is also capable of utter brilliance, dominating round after round with jaw-dropping consistency. The same goes for comedy—except you don't have a caddy telling you which jokes to use.

WHEN APTITUDE AND ATTITUDE COLLIDE

Not all funny people can become comics. To have a successful comedy career, you must possess a few necessary, maybe dull, traits—resilience, earnestness, tenacity, and adaptability ... But how do people realize they're funny to start with? Ten sorts of people attempt standup comedy.

1. Class clown

Class clowns have a captive audience—their classmates. Their disruptive humor often leads to banishment from the class. As adults, they fondly remember the thrill of the group laugh. Their desire to recapture that naughty tingle can lead them toward comedy.

2. Quiet kid who made adults laugh

Friends never understood their humor, but teachers, neighbors, and parents' friends thought they were hilarious. Their advanced intellect often made them feel superior to their peers. As adults, they simply know they're funny. They also realize not everyone feels the same way.

Are they laughing at me ... or with me?

3. Performer

Musicians, actors, and dancers often enter their field before discovering an intimate love of comedy. Singers get laughs during in-between-song banter. Actors enjoy improv more than working from scripts. Dancers may prefer pratfalls to pliés. Since they're already comfortable onstage, performers see a clear path into standup comedy paved with yucks.

4. Funniest person at work

This type is easily identified. Be it tales of weekend antics or devastating impressions of the manager (when not in earshot!), they hear "You should be a comedian!" so often, they start to think, "Hey ... maybe I could be a comedian." There's also a good chance they dislike their jobs.

5. Funny friend

Funny people tend to clump together socially. There always seems to be one person who can top every story, get to a punch line faster, or retell a story better than anyone else. Oddly, they're rarely the one who becomes the comic; it's the second funniest person in the circle who goes onstage—much to the dismay of Funny Person #1.

Did you sit in the back of the classroom or the front of the classroom? Just asking.

6. Adventurer

Some people want to cross everything off their to-do list. They don't usually have a lifelong desire to perform standup, but do seem up for a challenge. Adventurers enter "funniest teacher" contests or go onstage to celebrate their birthdays, while friends cheer them on.

7. Lifelong comedy fan

These fans listened to their parents' comedy albums or watched standup shows on television (often clandestinely) and knew they wanted to be comedians. It might have taken until adulthood to confess this yearning—to themselves and to others—but secretly they became focused on that goal. It's a calling.

Sometimes there's fierce competition among the folks in the immediate family! That which does not kill us makes us funnier.

9. The "I can do that" type

Some audience members watch a standup comic perform and think inwardly, "I can do that." Even if they have never before entertained the notion of going onstage, the feeling is magnetic and powerful.

8. Funniest in the family

Families often have one member (be it an aunt or younger sibling) who cracks everybody up at holiday gatherings. In a clan that values humor, this person is cherished. In a humorless family, this person is a disappointment or an annoyance. Both can be motivation for seeking a career involving the telling of jokes.

10. The others

Radio personalities, cruise directors, and motivational speakers are all up to their ears in comedy of some form. They may even tell jokes to a crowd as part of their daily duties. The desire to tell jokes in the more unstructured atmosphere of a comedy club can be alluring.

> Every comedian has a moment in his life when he realizes he's a bit different from everyone else. It's like being the only guy in a movie who sees the ghost. The ghost talks to you and you talk to him. Then you turn to your friend and say, 'Hey. Do you see that ghost?' And he says, 'What ghost?'
>
> Chris Roc

Reader, you may not fit into any of these categories. We do presume that you think you're funny, though. A sense of humor is crucial for doing standup.

"Dying is easy, comedy is hard"

When someone decides to focus on standup, they announce, "I want to try to do standup." Stating it that way allows for failure—there's an admission the experience may be unpleasant or even prove unachievable. Standup involves one of the top ten human fears; addressing a roomful of strangers is right up there with snakes, heights, needles, and being enclosed in a small space. While aspiring comics are attracted to the idea of making people laugh, they might also be intimidated by the prospect of "public speaking."

"Am I crazy? Am I totally insane? What was I thinking?" Don't worry. You're probably okay. Everyone else is nutty.

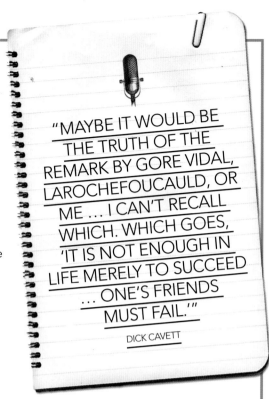

"MAYBE IT WOULD BE THE TRUTH OF THE REMARK BY GORE VIDAL, LAROCHEFOUCAULD, OR ME ... I CAN'T RECALL WHICH. WHICH GOES, 'IT IS NOT ENOUGH IN LIFE MERELY TO SUCCEED ... ONE'S FRIENDS MUST FAIL.'"

DICK CAVETT

Are you mad?

If you dare tell folks that you harbor strange comedy thoughts, their reaction goes something like this: "You want to mount a stage, bathed in light, and convince a mob you know what's funny?" Not unlike something a lion tamer or a high-wire act might receive—a mixture of awe, curiosity, and (maybe) a touch of admiration. Perhaps accompanied by a shudder ... Plus a dollop of envy. Were there a list detailing the top ten human desires, it would include the ability to amuse a roomful of strangers alongside being popular, attractive, and having piles of money.

DROPPING THE BOMB

Not everyone is going to be happy with your decision. Your parents would be ecstatic if you announced your intention to become a doctor or a professional athlete, or even an accountant. But a comedian? If you can deal with their dismay, you're well on your way to becoming a comic because dealing with disappointment is a very useful skill in one's early days as a comic. Comedians frequently "disappoint" a crowd once or twice, or 100 times … sometimes 100 times during a 45-minute set. This is called "bombing" (a quaint little term that colorfully describes utter failure).

Bad job

Let's face it: doing standup comedy is devilishly difficult, but if you thought doing it competently is challenging, imagine how hard it is to do it badly! If all goes according to the rules of nature, you will (at least at the start of your career) do standup comedy very, very badly. You will "die" onstage—another sweet little word for falling flat on your face, metaphorically speaking.

Let other folks do the worrying for you. After all, it's not them up there onstage enduring the silence.

Don't believe the hype

There have been stories of comedians who hit it off with their crowds at first try and proceed to skip merrily through a career in mirthmaking without one moment of awkward silence or a single nasty word from an audience member. These stories are apocryphal (otherwise known as simply untrue). You. Will. Bomb. It's nothing to be ashamed of, nor is it a sign that you were not meant to do standup comedy. If that were the case, 99.9 percent of all standup comics would not be standup comics. But be prepared to bomb. Do not fear the bomb; embrace the bomb; and learn from it. More later.

"QUISQUE COMOEDUS EST"

There's an old expression: "Everybody's a comedian." To get an idea of just how ubiquitous it is, some bright spark saw fit to translate it into a dead language for fun! The expression is usually muttered wearily, or hissed through clenched teeth, often with a roll of the eyes. It's a sarcastic statement, usually delivered after someone attempts (and often fails) to make a joke, sometimes at an inappropriate time or in an inappropriate location. "Comedians," especially amateur ones, are about as appreciated as dentists or skunks. But it's easy to avoid such opprobrium—choose your spots carefully. This doesn't mean "Keep your trap shut," but humor outside the context of a comedy club, and among strangers, is a tricky business. Tread lightly, be aware of your surroundings, use a modicum of caution. Even the chicken looked both ways before crossing the road.

Have you ever felt a peculiar kind of embarrassment when witnessing a grossly inappropriate human performance, such as the antics of an unfunny comedian? It is a depersonalized, almost metaphysical embarrassment at having to witness so undignified a behavior on the part of a member of the human species.

Ayn Rand

WHAT'S MY MOTIVATION?

We have a natural curiosity to discover why people act as they do, and this also extends to our fascination with comedians. There seems to be far too much theorizing: instead of just enjoying the comedy, people seem intent on finding out why it's being created. Much of the speculation focuses on the comedian's mental health. Surely, the reasoning goes, this person alone on the stage, bathed in light, eliciting laugh after laugh from a roomful of strangers must somehow be lacking something. They must be damaged.

Why me?

Others in the performing arts are rarely held up to such scrutiny. Singers sing, dancers dance, and actors act—and we're grateful that they do. But for some reason comics aren't allowed just to tell jokes. It's not feasible that they're actually telling jokes about sex, dogs, or airplanes. Instead, they must be dealing with repressed childhood trauma, resulting in feelings of insecurity and inadequacy—according to pop-Freudian theory. Maybe comedians become comedians because they can? Or, to paraphrase a quote famously attributed to Freud, "Sometimes a cigar joke is just a cigar joke."

You: "What did I do last night?" Them: "You did something I wouldn't do in a million years ... and you didn't do so bad!"

Tortured souls

Yes, there are comedians who are tortured, just as there are dancers, actors, brain surgeons, or postal workers who are emotionally tormented. But we seem to want to believe that the number of nutty comedians is disproportionately high. The fact that one or two high-profile comedians have been diagnosed with mental health issues, such as bipolar disorder, might help to perpetuate this image. Make no mistake—comedy can drive you crazy. But you don't have to be insane to want to try it.

The Joker is Wild (1957) detailed the alcohol-soaked life of singer–comedian Joe E. Lewis. Frank Sinatra's portrayal of the man, one of American comedy's biggest stars for three decades or so, was described at the time by *Variety* as "alternately sympathetic and pathetic, funny and sad."

For the first time I was surrounded by other people who actually believed that being funny could be a career … One day I was doing silly stuff at home to annoy my parents. The next I was getting paid to do it onstage. It was an exhilarating transition.

Tom Green

HOW TO GET STARTED

With a few rare exceptions, standup comedians start off in a show known as an "open mic night" (or "open mike"—both are abbreviations of "microphone"). They're also called open stage nights, amateur nights, or showcase nights … At least, that's the typical path to comedy competence in the modern era (1976 to present). By open mic, we mean a non-paying (or low-paying, for a lucky few) open stage show, usually on an off night at a comedy club, nightclub, bar, or coffee house, doing a short set (maybe three to eight minutes). Sometimes they're even held at an "alternative" venue, like a laundromat, library, or bookstore. There are other ways of going about it (comedy classes, improv classes, humor writing classes), but they invariably lead to the aforementioned open mic. (See Chapter 4 for more about classes.)

What are my odds?

You may be wondering: How competitive is standup comedy? What are my odds of success? How many comics will I be competing against? The answer: No one knows. It could be 2,000; it could be 5,000. It really doesn't matter— there are a lot of comedians out there, and what you have to do is figure out a way to make yourself stand out.

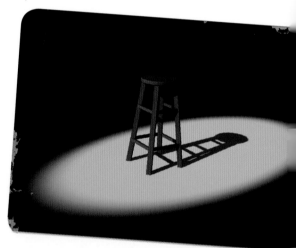

A day in the life

Comics who make a living in this biz have no typical day. They make ends meet in a variety of ways, and a large number travel from club to club, city to city, for many weeks of the year. This is probably how you imagine most comics operate … because this is how most comics operate! But it may be a good idea to broaden your idea of what a funny person might do to earn a decent wage. This way, you can save yourself a lot of time and frustration down the line. If you get a taste for the traveling life, and you like it, go for it.

"RATHER THAN HAVING SOMETHING TO FALL BACK ON, I WOULD SUGGEST STAYING AS DIVERSIFIED AS POSSIBLE. IF A DOOR SLAMS SHUT, TRY GOING THROUGH THE WINDOW. IF THE WINDOW IS CLOSED, TRY GOING THROUGH THE CELLAR."

RITA RUDNER

"CAN YOU ...?"

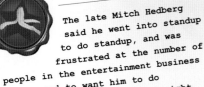

The late Mitch Hedberg said he went into standup to do standup, and was frustrated at the number of people in the entertainment business who seemed to want him to do something else besides. "All right. You do standup," he recounted, "but can you write?" An exasperated Hedberg followed up with, "This is not right. This is like if you were an excellent chef and somebody said to you, 'You're an excellent cook, but can you farm?'"

ROAD TO ANYWHERE

There are many different forks in the comedy road. Standup can lead to acting in movies, presenting on television, writing for radio, motivational speaking … or to more standup comedy. No matter what you do, there will be pressure—from a variety of angles—to do something else. Ultimately, it comes down to what you want to do. Discard the notion of a "typical" comic, and you'll have fewer constraints on what you do and how you achieve it.

Comedian Craig Ferguson is also an actor, an author, a screenwriter, a director, a musician, and a talk show host.

> The days of me being a highly regarded unknown by some were over. To be thought of as great but obscure is very poetic; to be a known comic who's had some breaks is a little less so.
>
> Mitch Hedberg

WORKING FOR A LIVING

You'll have an arsenal of double-edged swords at your disposal when you become a standup. Along with all the perks, there'll be corresponding responsibilities. You'll be self-employed, which entails a lot of freedom. Being your own boss means you'll have to be a model employee. Or, at least, you should be—there's nothing worse than having the boss angry at you, especially when you are the boss! If you're not a "self-motivated" sort, it may be better to investigate sketch comedy or an improv troupe; somewhere you can work within a group.

Keep track of those dates, organize those comedy notes, get to the gig on time, and keep focused on the goals!

Prince or pauper?

Expect to earn nothing. That way, you'll be pleasantly surprised when you make any money! Seriously, it is a lot like many other occupations. The potential for great reward is there for those who are willing to take risks, put in the hours, and gather and use their intelligence. In fact, there are fewer guarantees than in any other walk of life. This may sound like some sort of motivational speech from an adult continuing education class, but it's all true. Put in a less Tony Robbins kind of way, this is showbiz, kid.

See the light

Lately, there's been a lot of pontificating that sets forth exactly what a comic needs to do to be a good comic. If comics don't attain these goals, the logic goes that they don't deserve to call themselves comedians. For example, a comic isn't doing his or her job if he or she doesn't make audiences think. If a comic merely makes merry and fails to send everyone home with a moral, said comic is a disgrace to the corps, goes the thinking.

Such shortcomings, say the critics, are why standup comedy will never achieve the status of "art" and will fade into oblivion, along with other popular forms of entertainment like mahjong and flagpole sitting.

Chelsea Handler has had wild success in publishing, television, and personal appearances.

Claptrap

To say that comics must offer their audiences some kind of enlightenment is utter nonsense, and is a notion perpetuated by critics and sometimes (most embarrassingly) by comics themselves. Mind you, comedians shouldn't shy away from any attempt to enlighten, if that is their forte, but failure to follow that path does not make a comic any less of a comic, nor does it make Mr. or Mrs. Enlightenment any more of one.

WILL KILLING KILL ME?

Does all that traveling, performing, killing, bombing, and dying extend or curtail our life expectancy? Apparently, some pressure-filled situations can be good for our health. Scientists claim that a pressure-filled situation such as an occasional public-speaking gig can be advantageous to our health, and might delay the Grim Reaper. Apparently, when you're dying up there onstage, you're actually extending your life. Hmmm, maybe ...

Good stress/bad stress

Bad stress is chronic and uncontrollable, like the tension caused by an unhappy marriage or a sick relative. But there are lots of positives associated with short bursts of stress that ease up quickly, like being stuck in a traffic jam or sweating through a presentation to work colleagues. And what is standup if it isn't a sudden burst of stress that then fades away? Could this explain why so many comics live long, happy, healthy lives? George Burns lived to be 100, and he gigged to his last days!

Your parents told you to eat your broccoli ... they never told you to do your standup! Perhaps they had it all backward.

BABY COMEDIAN

Looking for "signs" you're fated to be a comic? Well, look no further than the annals of science. Scientific studies show that later-born siblings tend to be shorter and weigh less than their older siblings. They are also less likely to be vaccinated, are "looser cannons," less well educated, and less strapping than their older brothers and sisters. They're also more likely to live the (exhilarating) life of an artist or a comedian, adventurer, entrepreneur, GI, or firefighter. So all those years getting pounded on by your older siblings was actually Comedy Camp! This is a pretty good deal if you're an older child, as there's no reason to change. However, because younger siblings don't have size on their side, they initially struggle to shake things up, and one of the most effective strategies is humor. It's hard to resist someone who makes you laugh, and families abound with stories of last borns who are the clowns of the brood, and can get their own way simply by being funny or outrageous.

Funny youngies

Some of history's great satirists—Voltaire, Jonathan Swift, Mark Twain—were the youngest members of large families. Stephen Colbert, who yields to no one in his ability to get a laugh, often mentions that he's the last of 11 children. These examples may be little more than anecdotal, but personality tests show that, while first borns score especially well on the conscientiousness dimension (sense of general responsibility and follow-through), last borns score higher on "agreeableness," the simple ability to get along in the world.

Comedy actor Jim Carrey (here starring in *Bruce Almighty*, 2003) is the youngest of four siblings.

> I believe it is important for comedians to know who came before them. In fact, I believe comedians should know just about everything that came before them. As much experience, education, and awareness as one can attain is important.

Shelley Berman

RIM SHOT—RHYTHM AND TIMING

A "rim shot" is the sound you hear, played by the band's drummer, to accentuate the punch line of a joke. It's a cultural remnant, a leftover from the old vaudeville, burlesque, cabaret, or music hall shows, and survived through the middle of the twentieth century on television variety and talk shows. It pops up infrequently these days, and often is applied ironically. A proper rim shot, as we know it, consists of a strike on a snare drum, with a bit of the toms and a cymbal crash, and makes the onomatopoeic "Ba-dap-doom-dssh." Old-school comics also enlisted the pianist or horn player to accent certain physical bits with a tinkle of the keys or a "stab" of the trumpet. Modern comedians look upon such enhancements with contempt, seeing them as "comedy helpers" and definitely not in keeping with modern times.

> Standup is already an extremely diverse art form. We write, edit, direct, and perform. Most of us are booking and promoting, too. I do standup regularly, but I specialize in writing comedy. Most folks seem to end up specializing.
>
> Evan Da

TEARS OF A CLOWN

An enduring cultural idea is the comedian who is laughing on the outside but crying on the inside. The opera *Pagliacci* might be the culprit here. First performed in New York in 1893, the show has been a crowd favorite ever since. In it, Canio, in clown makeup, delivers a tearful showstopper. The image of a clown crying— oh, the irony!—has endured, not helped by the fact that Enrico Caruso's 1907 recording of the climactic "No Pagliaccio son non" was the first record to sell a million copies. Smokey Robinson and the Miracles gave the concept a boost when they released the multimillion seller "Tears of a Clown" in 1967, which referenced the weeping Pagliacci and reinforced the idea of a comedian with a dual nature:

"Just like Pagliacci did
I try to keep my surface hid
Smiling in the public eye
But in my lonely room I cry
The tears of a clown."

Are clowns really sad on the inside? Let's cut open a few dead ones and find out!

"ONE THAT ALWAYS ANNOYS ME IS THE MISCONCEPTION THAT STANDUP COMICS ARE ALWAYS 'ON.' FOR THE MOST PART THAT'S REALLY ONLY SHITTY COMICS THAT DO THAT. I DON'T KNOW ANY REALLY FUNNY COMICS THAT ARE ANNOYING AND CONSTANTLY TRYING TO BE FUNNY ALL THE TIME IN NORMAL CONVERSATION. THE ONES THAT DO THAT, WITHOUT EXCEPTION, USUALLY SUCK—AND PROBABLY STEAL."

JOE ROGAN

Everyone wants to be successful, but very few people want to continue working toward their goals. I can't tell you how many actors, writers, and comedians I know who won't let the past go. They obsess about the script that didn't sell, instead of working on a new script, or at least confronting their own inner demons that are blocking them from creating. If you want a career, you can't stop working on it. It sounds clichéd, but it's all about the process. Enjoy the results but keep going.

Evan Davis

FACE FOR COMEDY?

Believe it or not, there is such a thing as a comedy face. A group of scientists (obviously with too much time on their hands and a surfeit of money) set out to find the facial features that are most likely to induce laughter. They scanned and analyzed 179 facial features of 20 comedians' faces and concluded that the winning look—that of Ricky Gervais—was a combination of a round face, small forehead, wide nose, big lips, large eyes, and high cheekbones. The features most likely to mark male comedians out for success are essentially soft and feminine. The face is a strong indicator of character, and the study seemed to explain why comedians with a particular appearance would have been drawn to their careers.

Girly face

The characteristics of a feminine face suggest that the person may be agreeable and cooperative, and this helps us to form our first impressions of comedians as friendly and funny. Infants are preprogrammed to respond to the warmth and approachability of a mother's face, and in the same way, soft, feminine features put us at ease and encourage us to relax. This makes it easier for us to laugh and therefore to enjoy ourselves. Comedians need all the help they can get, so perhaps a face for comedy can make all the difference. Gervais' response to the news? "All these years I assumed my global success as a comedian was down to my acute observations, expert directorial rendering, and consummate skills as a performer. Turns out it's because I've got a fat, girly face."

Ricky Gervais' "fat, girly face" has led him to a fat, manly paycheck!

2
WHAT IS COMEDY?

It's a shame Plato was the first philosopher to devote any real brain power to the analysis of humor. Plato, it seems, blamed "comic" Aristophanes for the persecution and eventual execution of Socrates. Angered by the power of humor, Plato found little value in the pursuit of jokes. In the ensuing 2,400 years the examination of comedy has continued unabated. From Aristotle, to Hobbes, to Kant, to Freud, the joke has been scrutinized, studied, and probed to death. What each thesis has in common, however, is the eye-glazing dullness with which it is presented. We hope to avoid such dullness.

LAUGHING IS A LUXURY

Is laughter an "emotional luxury"? The dictionary defines a luxury as something that is desirable but not necessary. Certainly, there are benefits to laughter. It relieves tension, it feels good, it is also said to promote good health and prolong life ... even to cure cancer. People definitely seek it out. But do we really need it? If not, it might just be a luxury—at least, in modern times.

German philosopher Immanuel Kant said that laughter is "the sudden transformation of a tense expectation into nothing."

Cave humor

Way back when times were bad (say, for cave people), it could be that laughter was so rare it barely existed. Think about it. When you are in constant fear of your life, and death awaits at nearly every turn, when there is good reason to fear that dark and grisly death at the end of a tusk is a real possibility, maybe there simply wasn't a whole lot of laughing going on (or perhaps this was when comedy actually evolved ... see page 166).

Simply a perk?

Perhaps, as general conditions improved, humans became able to laugh. Or maybe it served some important, crucial purpose millions of years ago which shall forever remain a mystery. These days, though, it's vestigial—a nonessential extravagance that occasionally floods the brain with endorphins and distracts us from our inevitable death. One way of seeing whether laughter is necessary is to take a look at someone who doesn't laugh. Yes, such a person really does exist!

DELIVER THE PUNCH, THEN DUCK!

A study found that jokes that don't deliver humor violate a social contract. Therefore punishing the teller can discourage similar behavior in the future. This research doesn't seem very scientific, but at the heart of it there's something we have always maintained—folks get very hostile when their trust is violated in matters relating to humor, or if their funny bones aren't tickled.

There are very few people on the planet who don't know this or at least pick up on it at a subliminal level. How else to explain the reluctance of most to tell a joke in a social setting? The vast majority of people are loathe to tell a joke for fear of screwing it up. Why? Because they know that such a situation leads to ill will and embarrassment. On the other hand, anyone who excels at telling jokes tends to enjoy a certain cachet at work or at the bar.

Have an exit strategy... just in case they don't laugh.

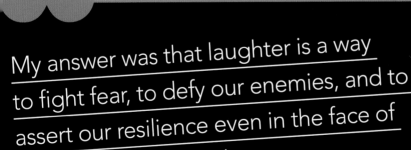

My answer was that laughter is a way to fight fear, to defy our enemies, and to assert our resilience even in the face of overwhelming tragedy.

Argus Hamilton

> # Comedy is defiance. It's a snort of contempt in the face of fear and anxiety. Laughter allows hope to creep back on the inhale.
>
> Will Durst

IS IT AN ADDICTION?

Endorphins are hormones found mainly in the brain that reduce pain sensation and affect one's emotions. They're really good drugs, but you don't need to visit the bad side of town to score some, because it's all manufactured, free of charge, in the folds of your gray matter! Just drop in a Benny Hill DVD, watch a Woody Allen movie, or pop into the nearest comedy club and watch a set or two …

Yeah, right!

Scientists also say that the same endorphins are released by running long distances or eating a hot pepper! Or so the story goes. As with so many physiological/psychological issues, there is some dispute. Whether these endorphins are released in significant enough amounts to make any difference, or to be addictive, is a matter of dispute even among those in the know.

Bipolar comic Ruby Wax, who has a degree in psychotherapy, took her musical comedy show on a tour of British mental health facilities. "If depressives laugh, you know you've got a hit," she says.

An addiction without a downside?

If it is an addiction, it's certainly one with no obvious downside. We've never heard of anyone overdosing on Russell Brand or failing to come into work because they've binged on Monty Python reruns. And humor "junkies" looking for their next "fix" are rarely, if ever, caught stealing a television or nodding off in a corner.

I want it now!

It doesn't matter whether we need laughter or not—we want it, we can afford it, and we can get it in vast quantities. What's more, you might be one of those people who can provide it. But how? To whom? And where? And why? These are all very good questions. Let's attempt to answer them.

First question—What is comedy?

"LAUGHTER IS A CHEAP DRUG. A JOKE IS A CLEAN NEEDLE."

BRIAN MCKIM

LAUGHTER IS A DRUG

Researchers at Stanford University claim that a comic cartoon fires up the same part of the brain as a line of cocaine. People were asked to select funny newspaper cartoons while the researchers looked at MRI scans of their heads. It seems the cartoons activated the same brain circuits as cocaine or money. Earlier investigations found that humor triggers the brain regions that analyze a joke's language and meaning, or those that control smiling and laughter. This finding may help to diagnose early stages of depression (a time when people's sense of humor changes), or to show if someone's antidepressants are working.

AMBIENT HUMOR: HUMOR THAT ... EXISTS

Humor is anything that makes us laugh or smile, even if it's a quiet, satisfied smile on the inside. There doesn't have to be an outward indication that it has amused us. Sometimes the humor wasn't meant to make us laugh—it just did. Sometimes it's not instantly humorous, and it only reveals itself as funny after considerable thought or analysis. We like to call such instances "ambient humor." Here are some examples:

- A dog chasing his tail
- A child innocently saying something funny
- An obscenely shaped cactus by the side of the road.

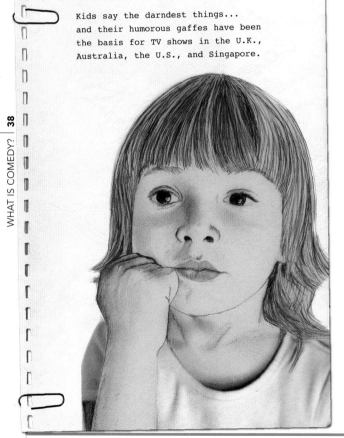

Kids say the darndest things... and their humorous gaffes have been the basis for TV shows in the U.K., Australia, the U.S., and Singapore.

Found humor

Neither the dog, nor the child, nor the cactus, set out to make us giggle. Here we're dealing with "found humor." It's really up to the observer to recognize the humor, and for him or her to translate it so that other people can start laughing.

Whatever it takes

The examples above are humor, but what we do with it is the joke. Comedians need to use all means at their disposal to create a joke. It has to evoke laughter, and can appear in many forms— as an anecdote, a sketch, a prop, a song, a pantomime, a script for a television show, a photograph ... Basically, this is comedy.

> "NOTHING IS MORE CURIOUS THAN THE ALMOST SAVAGE HOSTILITY THAT HUMOR EXCITES IN THOSE WHO LACK IT."
>
> GEORGE SAINTSBURY, ENGLISH WRITER AND CRITIC

IF A TREE FALLS IN THE WOODS, AND NO ONE HEARS IT, IS IT FUNNY?

You've observed something you think is humorous, and now you set out to create some sort of joke. Remember that every joke needs a speaker and a listener. In most cases, aspiring comedians seek to entertain people at a comedy club, working men's club, or at an open mic or amateur night. They don't get to choose their audience or its demographic makeup. (Though they can be reasonably certain that, generally speaking, such venues will contain men and women between the ages of 21 and 65!)

Pryor is cited by many comics as their number one influence.

RICHARD PRYOR AND BILLY CONNOLLY: CHAMPIONS

Two unscientific polls (one by U.S. cable outlet Comedy Central; the other by independent U.K. network Channel 4) tried to determine the greatest comedian of all time. Richard Pryor topped the U.S. list, while Scottish comic Billy Connolly was voted number one in the U.K.

Far from being a piece of intellectual frippery—comedy is the most powerful art form known to man. I have seen a few ballets and not one of them has induced me to question anything other than the nature of thighs.

Brian Hennigan

> "Comedy is underrated … When you tell a joke, people either laugh, or they don't. The way to gauge success is straightforward. In a play, it's not so easy to tell if your audience is with you or not.
>
> Simon Pegg

HUMOR IS SUBJECTIVE

In addition to "Git 'er done," comedian Dan Whitney (a.k.a. "Larry the Cable Guy") has a second catchphrase—"I don't care who you are, that's funny right there." Larry insists that some jokes or situations may actually be universally funny. Even though the Cable Guy might insist otherwise, humor really is subjective.

"One of the hardest parts of my job is figuring out what other people will think is funny."
Scott Adams, creator of Dilbert.

Funniest joke in the world?

If we can't even agree on what's funny, this makes it hard to analyze humor. And we can rule it out as a military weapon. "The Funniest Joke in the World," a Monty Python sketch from 1969, depicted the absurd notion of a joke that was so funny that those who heard it died laughing. It therefore contradicted the notion that comedy is an individual matter.

Room at their fingertips

Isn't this what all comedians strive for—concocting a joke that (while not fatal) will be so universal that everyone who hears it will laugh heartily? Even if we could account for differences in language, culture, politics, age, and class, we still couldn't dream up a joke that would achieve this. That is why evoking laughter from a random roomful of people—even from a sliver of that room—is such a tall order. It also explains why those who can pull it off are seen as possessing a magical skill.

Vital ingredients

Comedians need to recognize humor when they see it, and then be able to capture the essence of that humor and convey it to others so that they, too, may see it. This is the very essence of comedy.

BAD DAY AT THE OFFICE

Ricky Gervais got into hot water for some of the jokes he told while hosting the 2011 Golden Globes. He was roundly "condemned" by various "offended" groups. Initially (and unofficially) the Hollywood Foreign Press Association expressed outrage, hinting that he would never host the show again. It eventually issued the following statement: "We loved the show. It was a lot of fun and obviously has a lot of people talking … Certainly, in this case, [Ricky] pushed the envelope and occasionally went too far … Overall, however, the show was among the best we've ever had and we were pleased."

Awards shows and banquets hire comedians with a history of saying the most outrageous things about the most famous people, and when the comedians proceed to do exactly that, the powers-that-be talk to the press, expressing varying degrees of disgust, anger, or surprise. David Letterman, Jon Stewart, and Chris Rock had similar experiences while hosting the Academy Awards ceremony.

"EVERYONE HAS A SENSE OF HUMOR. A LOT OF THINGS THAT SOME PEOPLE FIND FUNNY, OTHER PEOPLE JUST DON'T FIND FUNNY … THAT'S WHY YOU HAVE SOMEBODY WHO WILL SAY, 'GEE, I THINK LAUREL AND HARDY ARE WONDERFUL,' AND SOMEBODY ELSE WILL SAY, 'THEY STINK. I DON'T UNDERSTAND THEM.'"

JOHNNY CARSON

IT'S A CULTURAL THING

It might be because of basic cultural differences, but what you find funny may not be funny to someone on the other side of the world, because ... well, just because ... Or it could be that two cultures have developed along different paths. Certain quirks, twists, and turns of history have brought certain inhabitants of the planet to a different place—a place where we laugh at radically different things.

Technology helps!

How far has humor infiltrated the culture? Since the middle of the nineteenth century, North America, the U.K., and Australia have all had mass-circulated, English-language books and magazines, lectures, music halls, theaters, universities, vaudeville, burlesque, and—more recently—television, movies, DVDs, VHS, Betamax, and radio to accelerate the comedy smorgasbord and stir up the mix.

Humor has accelerated the growth and adaptation of new technology since the invention of movable type. The Internet was no exception.

I'M SORRY!

Type "apologized for a joke" into Google and you get a LOT of hits. Everyone from Oscar-winner Halle Berry to fashion designer Kenneth Cole to golf champion Fuzzy Zoeller to U.S. President Barack Obama have felt compelled to publicly apologize for an attempt at humor that was deemed offensive to an individual or a group. Some survive the incident with their careers intact, but others do not. Clearly, for sports figures, actors, and politicians (and others), trying to appear witty and humorous is fraught with danger.

Exploding boundaries

It may be true that the musings of Mark Twain or Stephen Leacock might still be appreciated by 21st-century readers (and may be viewed by those same readers as timeless). Boxed sets of Laurel and Hardy movies might well be laughed at by successive generations of comedy fans. It may even be accurate to say that Will Rogers or Abraham Lincoln are viewed as witty and eloquent storytellers or political commentators. But the boundaries of humor are ever-expanding.

So popular was German comedian, actor, and poet Heinz Erhardt that he was immortalized on a stamp on the occasion of the 100th anniversary of his birth.

Humor can be dissected, as a frog can, but the thing dies in the process and the innards are discouraging to any but the pure scientific mind.

E. B. White

NEVERENDING CIRCLES

As a culture advances, so does its humor progress. And, as the humor expands, the definition of what counts as funny does as well. The more connected a people are, the more they will marinate in mass media, and the more shared or common experiences they will have. Common experience is vital to the advance of the comedy vanguard, because the more connected everyone is, the greater the number of people who will "get the joke." And, once folks have figured out the joke, they will then seek out the next one. Wired, connected people have an insatiable appetite for humor. There's a lot of "churn" involved.

Humor aids in socialization
(acquiring a personal identity and
learning the norms, values, behavior,
and social skills appropriate to
one's social position).

DANGER IS COMEDY'S MIDDLE NAME

In an episode of *South Park*, Matt Stone and Trey Parker depicted the prophet Mohammed wearing a bear suit. Shortly thereafter, Zachary Adam Chesser (a.k.a. Abu Talhah al-Amrikee) issued a fatwa against the producers of the show, threatening their lives in the name of Islam. Chesser later pled guilty to three felonies: communicating threats to Parker and Stone, soliciting violent jihadists to desensitize law enforcement, and attempting to provide material support to a designated foreign terrorist organization. In the U.S., these are all offenses punishable by as much as 30 years in prison. A few days later, a gas bomb capable of killing a few hundred people in every direction was placed within a few yards of the building housing the corporation that owns Comedy Central. Months later, Faisal Shahzad was sentenced to life imprisonment without the possibility of parole after pleading guilty to a 10-count indictment, including charges of conspiracy to use a weapon of mass destruction and attempting an act of terrorism. He never said that he was aiming to blow up Comedy Central.

The duo almost wound up like Dutch director Theo van Gogh, i.e., shot eight times, stabbed in the chest, and nearly beheaded!

"We are the healers. We are the fourteenth-century barbers leeching them of their dread. We make people laugh out loud against their will. It's an honorable profession. Do it any way you can. Make people forget the outside world. I just do it different. Not better. Not worse. Different.

— Will Durst

OBVIOUS HUMOROUSNESS?

Who said "Humor is tragedy plus time"? It's been variously attributed to Woody Allen, Carol Burnett, Lenny Bruce, and Mark Twain, but our money's on Twain. Basically, you can make jokes about tragic incidents or circumstances, but you may need to hold off a little bit until the pain dissipates. This isn't exactly profound.

It's all in the timing

"Tragedy," in its loosest sense, often evokes laughter. It can be as simple as someone slipping on a banana peel (a comedy "classic") but can also reach as far as the Holocaust. A person slipping on a banana peel will bring on instant laughter, but for a horrific event like a mining disaster, or the passing of a beloved public figure, we might need to wait a long time until large numbers of people will be moved to laugh or feel that laughter is appropriate.

We asked a scientist: "What are the odds of slipping on a banana peel?" His reply: "First: Do you own a monkey?"

Tread carefully

In any tragedy, there might be elements of absurdity, irony, incongruity, or coincidence, all of which have the potential to trip the laughter response. But other factors surrounding tragic events can often obliterate any laughs. It is best to exercise caution when mining tragedy as a source of comedy. Figuring out just how much time must pass is a delicate calculation.

WHEN HUMOR HUMILIATES

In the mid-1990s, a new social phobia was recognized: a debilitating fear of being laughed at, called **gelotophobia**. Simply being in the company of others having fun and laughing can induce extreme tension and apprehension for some people. Gelotophobes are not able to understand the positive side of humor, nor can they experience it in a warm way (rather, as a means to put others down). Willibald Ruch, from the University of Zurich, says that those who work with groups of people should acknowledge that humor is not universally contagious. He says that teased kids who show up at school the next day with a gun might be reacting to an inability to react to the teasing with good humor, and that these gelotophobic children are the ones with the problem!

There's also the flip side—those who suffer from **katagelasticism**, a condition describing people who enjoy laughing at others to excess. Hopefully, most of us fall nicely in the middle of the two!

Through the use of microexpressions (brief, involuntary facial expressions), we grant or revoke permission to laugh.

Gallows humor

There are some people—doctors, police officers, soldiers, for instance—who engage in so-called "gallows" or "morbid" humor. Context is very important in these cases. Quite often, those who deal with death, destruction, and treachery on a regular basis may be inured to it, and they may mine the darker side of human nature for humor. It is a coping mechanism and, with rare exceptions, such humor is not fit for general consumption.

Laughing in the face of death is a perfectly normal thing to do. We can assume that Death is not a fan of such activity.

I could have died …

What of the ultimate tragedy: our own death? We all die. None of us can escape it. This may be why so many jokes, either implicitly or explicitly, hinge on our mortality. Jokes that touch on experiences that are common to the greatest number of people have the best chance of causing mirth, so poking fun at your eventual demise isn't as grim as it sounds. "Laughing in the face of death" often refers to bravery, but we all laugh in the face of death—in little ways and in large ways, in significant ways and insignificant ones. And sometimes we do so unwittingly.

SARCASM AND DEMENTIA

People with frontotemporal dementia (FTD) are often reported as being humorless and lacking a sense of irony. An Australian study from 2003 claimed that those with the disease find it hard to read emotions and cannot sense when someone is being sarcastic. This is significant, because if caregivers are angry, sad, or depressed, patients will not pick this up, and this is often very upsetting for family members. FTD is often misdiagnosed as a personality disorder. We may value a sense of humor so highly, and deem it so important, that those who lack one are considered rude and distant, and we ostracize them. Who would have thought sarcasm would figure in a study of mental illness? Getting the joke—picking up on sarcasm—might be a key of being "normal."

George Carlin's 13th HBO special, entitled "Life Is Worth Losing," dealt with suicide, violence, and the human condition.

OLDER FOLKS DON'T GET THE JOKES

Or, as the eggheads put it: "Further study of humor comprehension is warranted because of the potential physical and psychological benefits of humor." To put it yet another way, scientists have studied the different ways that old folks "get" a joke and compared these to the way younger people understand them. They concluded that, not only are there differences but, because humor is so important, we should investigate exactly why these discrepancies occur. Again, science regards humor (and the comprehension of humor) as very important—not just because it's good to laugh. It seems that discovering why we laugh may also be significant, and finding out why some folks lose the ability to laugh may provide insight into other areas of psychological study. So ... humor is a very serious business.

OLDIES BUT GOLDIES?

A 2007 study aimed to understand factors relating to humor comprehension in old age. It claimed that older adults find it more difficult to understand humor, as a result of age-related cognitive decline. The researchers administered a range of tests and discovered that older adults tended to score lower on tests of humor and cognitive abilities. They suggested that there may be age-related deficits in humor comprehension, which need further study because of humor's potential physical and psychological benefits.

Older folks who seek out comedy clubs contradict the stats in these studies. Do not use these studies as permission to dismiss a white-haired crowd ... or a white-haired comedian.

WE LOSE IT AT 52

Some scientists set out to discover when we stop laughing, and concluded that we lose our sense of humor—on average—at the age of 52. Of course, your mileage may vary.

Might this be a function of culture? Or of history? In subsequent generations, will this figure rise or fall? If they'd carried out the study in 1950, what would the average age have been—higher or lower?

BABIES SMILING IN THE WOMB

Babies, it appears, can smile at birth, or even sooner—ultrasounds have actually spotted upside-down frowns on babies in the last three months of pregnancy. What is unclear is why they do it so early on. Research shows that they often smile when they're falling asleep or waking up (times that are frequently pleasurable for babies).

Social smiling—when a baby breaks into a gummy grin as a response, for example, to a familiar face or the start of a favorite activity—doesn't occur until around two months. By the time a baby reaches 3 to 4 months, he or she can smile so broadly that his or her cheekbones lift up, and may laugh.

So we laugh even before we're born. And we continue to guffaw (with the exception of a brief respite during our sullen teen years) until we're 52!

3
BASICS OF WRITING FUNNY

You can't go a day, maybe not even an hour, without encountering some form of humor. It's everywhere: on the television or radio, in the newspaper, in motion pictures, on the Internet, in greeting cards, books, calendars, live presentations, CDs, cell phone applications, advertising … Wherever you look, there's a joke of some kind, specially written to elicit a smile, laugh, guffaw, an LOL, ROFL, or LMAO. And each gag has been crafted by someone who knows "how to write funny," and has its origin in its own special writing place, be it a booth in a diner or a desk in a high-rise office building. Learning to write funny might lead to performing to a crowd of thousands at Wembley, or it may simply liven up your annual family newsletter. Most likely, it'll fall somewhere between these two, but relatively few people possess the skill.

FLIP A SWITCH

Condition your brain to think more like a comedian. Some people find the process easier than others—they're probably already huge fans of a comic movie star or have memorized lines from television sketches, or even tried parodying a pop hit. Others need a nudge. If you aren't already gobbling up as much comedy as you can, get going now! Go back and see your favorite comedian, or watch a beloved television comedy, but this time observe the performance as a comedy student, not a fan. Figure out what makes it work. If you've never thought you could write comedy, give it a try. You are now a producer of humor, not a consumer.

Check your comedy inventory

It might feel odd analyzing your repertoire, methods, and strengths, but it is crucial to be introspective. Taking a humor inventory plays a part in training the brain to produce comedy on demand, and developing a way of creating rather than just leaving it to chance. Look at your musings, written essays, or blog posts, and work out what made them humorous. If you've recently made an elevator full of strangers laugh, or had a gaggle of co-workers in stitches, examine what it was that "worked" and what didn't.

There's tons of comedy on the Internet ... you don't even have to leave your laptop to find a laugh!

Dissecting your writing doesn't have to destroy spontaneity—but it is necessary. To recreate comedy gold moments you must examine what made them funny in the first place. Strike a balance between spontaneity and deliberateness. Observe your own everyday "performance"—how you interact with friends or colleagues—just as you would that of your favorite performer. Ask whether a future delivery of the joke would yield the same results. Friends may have laughed because they know you, so you need to question whether a room full of strangers would react similarly. Would people without "inside" knowledge of a gag be amused? Funny people spend hours editing and reimagining their jokes in this way.

Undercover operation

The strangers or co-workers serving as test audiences for your "hilarious" vacation disaster story shouldn't realize they are your comedy lab rats, nor should you ask for feedback (their laughter will suffice). Don't take it out on them if you fail to elicit hoots of laughter, and don't be obnoxious. If, after some introspection, you think you have what it takes to actively attempt to amuse others, you have no other choice but to make the leap. Remember that stealth comedy on unsuspecting "victims" is very different from naked attempts to amuse.

Unquestionably, standup comedy is and has always been an art form. It is a form of theatrical presentation. The writing of material and the execution of it—exactly as playwright and actor—is obviously a creative endeavor.

Shelley Berman

TEAM UP?

Scriptwriters, performers, and comics often have partners they can "bounce ideas off." The actual writing of humor need not necessarily be a solo endeavor, and it's often immensely helpful to work with someone who shares your sensibilities, experiences, or points of reference. They can serve as a built-in test audience, enabling lightning-fast tweaking and rewriting of jokes or routines. Aside from the practical aspects, it makes the creative process less solitary.

WRITER VS. PERFORMER

Modern standup performers are predominantly also writers—the singer–songwriters of the comedy world. Very little purchasing of material goes on among comics except at the higher levels of the business, and very few writers can make a living selling material to multiple comedians. Because of their position as television show hosts or presenters, or due to heavy personal/television appearance schedules, some performers purchase material and rely on a staff of writers or a handful of freelancers.

But not all comedy writers want to be performers. Some start out as performers but gradually give up the spotlight to concentrate on writing or directing, while others find their way onto the stage or in front of the camera. Some are perfectly happy never to leave their keyboards. The comedy writing business is quite fluid, and it isn't a decision for life. Comedy writers may also discover they're not good at writing all types of comedy—the brilliant standup comic may turn out to be a horrible novelist; the syndicated columnist may be unable to churn out a readable script; and radio writers may fail miserably when translating their humor to television.

Larry David teamed with Jerry Seinfield in 1989 to co-create the series *Seinfield*, where he also acted as head writer and executive producer.

BUYING MATERIAL

For a new comic, buying material is pointless. If you want to speak other people's words, become an actor. Writing your own comedy is crucial to discovering what kind of comedian you are. It is acceptable to use the occasional joke written by somebody else—a fellow comic, best friend, audience member (with permission, of course)—but if you buy most of your act when you're just starting out, maybe you should be doing something else.

Peter Cook and Dudley Moore created "Derek and Clive" to distinguish their X-rated sketches from their wholesome "Pete and Dud" material.

BE ORIGINAL

Occasionally your material may be eerily similar to something written by another comic. Often it's just a matter of parallel development—two people having the same idea. If a political leader is caught in a sex scandal, for instance, it's quite likely another person will come up with the same joke. That's why it's important, especially early on, to know what came before you and what's going on now. The only way to guarantee a joke's originality is to tell a story from your own life, the theory being that if it happened to you it can't have happened to anybody else. Somebody else will tell you if you're doing another comedian's joke. Always try to be scrupulously original.

Taking notes in the back of a comedy club, then doing material based on those notes is not original comedy.

Stealing

Nothing damages a career in standup, or any other comedy-related industry, as much as misappropriating material. *Caveat emptor*: know the source of your material. Unscrupulous characters will sell you material that did not originate with them, and this is one more reason why novice comics and writers shouldn't purchase jokes. Some open-micers go on stage for the first time and do an entire chunk of material from a famous comedian. This is wrong. You don't have permission to speak the words of Bill Cosby, Rita Rudner, or Bill Hicks, so don't use their material. It's that simple. Nor do you have the right to use jokes written by fellow open-micers or out-of-town comics, who you assume you'll never see again. Some comics will do another comic's joke, and then excuse themselves, saying they were "in the moment" and didn't realize what they were saying. This is nonsense. Stealing other people's material will haunt you for your entire career. Nobody likes a joke thief, so don't do it.

"The trick to writing topical comedy is twofold. First, you have to understand the news story well enough to know what's really going on, as opposed to what the news makers say is going on. Second, you have to know how much the audience knows about the story, because puzzled people don't laugh."

Argus Hamilton

DON'T BE A HACK

The worst thing anyone can accuse a comic of is being a "hack." The most devastating word you can use to describe a comedian's work is to label it "hack" (or, in rare cases, "hacky"). "Hack" is an adjective and a noun and it has a precise and subtle meaning (see below). A bit of clarification is in order: The word "hack" has recently evolved into a verb meaning "to steal." This would be wrong. After all, we already have a word for stealing: "stealing!" In any event, it's not a good thing to be called a hack. But it is possible to guard against becoming a hack. So, while it may not be useful or productive to call someone a hack, it is prudent to be constantly aware of whether or not you're producing hack material.

Dictionary corner

Open the dictionary. Under the word "hackneyed," we find "hackneyed, adj: lacking in freshness or originality" and under "hack," we find this: "hack, noun: a person who works solely for mercenary reasons; esp.: a writer working solely for commercial success." So a hack is a writer who churns out hackneyed material. Calling someone a "hack" is one of the more serious charges one comic can level at another; few things strike more directly at a comic's heart. If you don't intend to distinguish yourself in significant ways from other artists, what's the point in trying to create art? Before you toss around the "hack" accusation, make sure it's appropriately used, and spend it wisely.

ANOTHER TACK

If you can't help yourself, try this. When confronted with an act that tempts you to use such a characterization, instead attempt to find other things you don't like about this person's act or presentation. You might find out that the object of your distaste isn't a hack so much as an act that merely rubs you the wrong way or just doesn't float your boat.

Flying high?

Jokes that center on the experience of flying in an airplane have been deemed to be hack. During the comedy boom of the late twentieth century, thousands of comedians were flying (and millions of audience members also flew), so it was quite natural that they'd use this common experience for humor.

The problem is: a lot of comics started doing the same jokes as their colleagues. To be sure, some of this was due to thievery, but some of it was just coincidental. An example:

"When there's a plane crash, they look for the black box. It contains a recording of the pilots' conversation with the tower and it's encased in a material that can survive a plane crash. Question: Why don't they make the entire plane out of that material?"

Now, someone got to that joke first. And it's a darn fine, if perhaps somewhat obvious, observation that some people can take pride in having written. However, that particular joke and variations of it were declared to be "hacky," and, as such, were determined to be off-limits for any comic wishing to be seen as serious and original. This declaration was made arbitrarily and spread through some sort of professional osmosis until one day it was clear to every comedian on the planet.

There's a problem any time a topic or a premise is proscribed, as it limits what comics can or should talk about. It prevents a future comic from writing what might be the most wonderful and original airplane joke ever. It may be okay to declare a particular punch line to be played out or lacking in originality. (And there might often be clear evidence that it is ubiquitous and less than fresh.) But care must be taken to separate the punch line from the premise. If one declares a premise or a topic to be off limits, then artists are unnecessarily hemmed in.

It goes without saying that artists should always be examining their work and on high alert for items or works that might be less than fresh. But it should be an internal matter and not one that is imposed arbitrarily from without.

Were songwriters to labor under the same constraints, they would never write another love song. Novelists pressured in a similar fashion by their colleagues would refrain from writing another murder mystery or detective novel. Chefs wouldn't cook with chicken. And we'd all be poorer for it.

SELLING YOUR MATERIAL

If you don't want to perform—but definitely want to write comedy—try selling your material. More established comics may be looking for extra jokes, and it's fine to approach them at comedy clubs to see if they are interested in purchasing material. Don't randomly approach a load of different comics with the same jokes; wait till you find one with a similar sense of humor. Have a batch of 10 to 12 jokes at the ready—this suggests you can probably provide more material. Prepare to be rejected; far more comics don't buy than do.

An awful lot of material is written while alone, and possibly while sitting in a chair. Keep that notepad handy!

Writer's Market

Many comics solicit jokes via the *Writer's Market*, which (for a subscription fee) offers a hard copy and online version. It spells out how many jokes to submit and how much is paid per joke, etc., and writers are often asked to sign a confidentiality agreement. As well as comedians, comic strip writers, greeting card companies, and in-flight magazines solicit comedy material. Specs are provided, and often an editor or publisher details how to increase the odds of a sale. It's a good confidence-builder and you may pick up some cash. If you're not sure your jokes are worth selling, give a few to other comics to perform—this gives you a chance to see what works.

TV HEE HEE

Another option is to submit monologue jokes to television hosts. In America, at least, almost all shows use a number of freelance jokes. Just call up the show and ask about their procedure for submitting material.

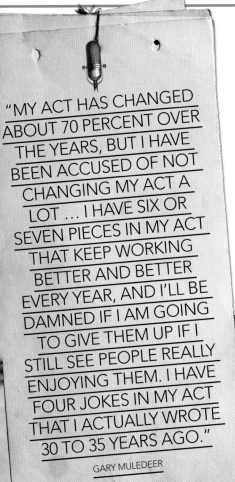

"MY ACT HAS CHANGED ABOUT 70 PERCENT OVER THE YEARS, BUT I HAVE BEEN ACCUSED OF NOT CHANGING MY ACT A LOT ... I HAVE SIX OR SEVEN PIECES IN MY ACT THAT KEEP WORKING BETTER AND BETTER EVERY YEAR, AND I'LL BE DAMNED IF I AM GOING TO GIVE THEM UP IF I STILL SEE PEOPLE REALLY ENJOYING THEM. I HAVE FOUR JOKES IN MY ACT THAT I ACTUALLY WROTE 30 TO 35 YEARS AGO."

GARY MULEDEER

HARVARD CONNECTION

Between graduating from Harvard and ascending to the host spot on NBC's Late Night eight years later, Conan O'Brien spent several years as a writer/producer for shows such as *Not Necessarily the News*, *The Simpsons*, and *Saturday Night Live*. While at the university, he served as president of the *Harvard Lampoon*. Several *Lampoon* alumni were on the staff of *The Simpsons*, *Late Show*, and other comedy shows, while most of *Monty Python* attended Cambridge or Oxford. Many prominent writers and performers hold degrees from prestigious institutions, but it's definitely not necessary to succeed in comedy.

Cambridge? Oxford? Harvard? Maybe. But it's not a prerequisite. Conan O'Brien went through Harvard on his way to TV fame.

> My material turns over glacially. I tell stories. I get good stories and I like to tell them. My first Tonight Show spot was one seven-minute story. It takes a while to put together a good story like that.
>
> Tom Parks

GETTING STARTED

If there was one particular joke that made you think you could write comedy, use it as your foundation: write others on the same subject or with the same rhythm. It can give you tremendous insight into your sense of humor and writing style. Some people don't have that "one joke," so have no idea how to get started. Comedy experts have suggested formulas designed to help beginning writers find their comedic writing style, which may initially seem helpful but risk making you sound like everybody else. Start writing by starting to write. Then rewrite and edit.

Write. Rewrite. Edit. Write again. Rewrite again. Most of what you write will be awful. So what!

THE HOOK

"Hooks" tie material together thematically, serving as convenient focal points for marketing or merchandising. Practically speaking, they allow fans to remember a comedian. Often a hook will be deeper than a phrase. In the case of Tim Allen, it's an entire point of view or concept—one that celebrates manhood and mines the familiar territory of sex differences. For good measure, a second hook—consisting of a series of primal grunts—is so recognizable and effective that it's used as a ringtone! Allen's clear P.O.V. was parlayed into a successful American television sitcom that ran for eight seasons.

Self-writing jokes?

Occasionally, jokes "write themselves," and just pop into your brain, fully formed. When performed for the first time, they work marvelously—with no need for alteration—and continue to do so with each retelling. There are other jokes, however, that do not. These need further examination, prodding, and reworking. You'll probably spend much of your time working on this second type … which is why learning how to rewrite is vital.

prose, try writing topical gags. Write a punch line to the top stories of the day, then watch talk show monologues to see how your jokes compare. Start a blog. Tweet. Write a funny Facebook status. Feedback from readers/followers/friends could prove invaluable.

Re-re-rewrite

Write a 500-word humorous essay. The next day, rewrite it. On the third day, rewrite it again. Do this for an entire week … or two. When you're done, you may have a much-improved 1,500-word essay or a single great joke, or something to throw in the garbage. Initially, at least, the process is more important than the outcome. If you prefer single jokes to lengthy

Fortunately, the days of a wastepaper basket filled with crumpled paper are gone! Hit delete and start over again!

RULES NOT TO BREAK

Comedy writing may be freewheeling, but there are laws, conventions, and rules of comedy nature that one needs to adhere to. These conventions are often harsh, yet they are necessary.

Punch line

Position it at the end of your joke. The most important word in the punch line goes right at the very end.

Balance

If you're going to have a long setup, make sure the punch line is worth it. Conversely, if the punch line is not particularly strong, keep the setup short. It might be a letdown for the audience, otherwise!

Rule of threes

Things are funnier when grouped in threes—it's an unwritten law. Perhaps it goes back to when we were babies and our parents tossed us up in the air, saying, "One, two, threeeeeee!" We expect to be delighted when the third item arrives.

Premise

A premise is an idea, not a joke (see page 172). To get a decent laugh, you need

Did we say "Rule" of threes? Sorry. Feel free to break this rule, too. But don't say we didn't warn you.

to do more with the premise than just draw attention to it. If it doesn't have a punch line, or isn't elaborated upon in some fashion, it's not a joke, just an observation. A premise can lead to one joke or many.

Obscure topics

Your audience won't understand a joke if they're not familiar with the topic, so explain it to them—and keep it entertaining (don't just spew out a load of facts and figures)! Humor that draws on the shared, everyday experiences of audience members gets right to the punch line quickly. When tackling topics like driving to work or dealing with a sales clerk, no explanation is needed, but more setup is needed for material that strays far from your audience's daily experiences (see Balance, on previous page).

Wordplay and puns

Jokes dealing with wordplay or puns must be extremely clever; otherwise, they can sound like jokes told in the schoolyard. This is not to say that you should avoid wordplay or puns—just tread carefully to avoid this pitfall.

66

There are big differences ... So many American comics fail in the U.K. because they insist on doing what they do here. And it just doesn't work. They have a different view of life ... Different ways, different perception of things. I had to hang around and rewrite things to fit. And, yes, I was very nervous the first time I did the U.K. but not as much working Australia. They are close [to Americans] in my mind.

Steve McGrew

99

YOU ARE WHO YOU ARE!

Comedy writers are often confronted with questions such as: Clean or dirty? One-liners or storytelling? Lowest common denominator or oddball? Early on, they choose a path and focus on it—often less an aesthetic choice, and more a means of survival, a way to focus one's output. If you try to be all things to all people, you may end up being nothing to no one.

All trades mastered?

Renaissance types, who display proficiency in a wide variety of styles or disciplines, do exist, but they are rare. Once in a (great) while, standup comics possess the discipline to have two, or three, radically different sets, making them prepared for nearly any occasion. For the most part, though, comedians make a decision, stick with it, and settle on a style and pace that suits their sensibilities, personality, and work ethic.

Florence Foresti's one-woman shows are inspired by her own life. The first show was about her single life as a 20-year-old Parisian; her second one was made after having a child and on what motherhood feels like. Her humor is very contemporary and people can easily relate to it.

NOT AGAIN?

"Can you believe it?" says Comic In The Back Of The Room #1. "He's still doing that lion tamer bit?! I saw him do that in 1991 on 'Evening at the Improv'"! C.I.T.B.O.T.R. #2 says, "It's time he got a new act!"

JUDD APATOW

Judd Apatow is a 20-year overnight success. Newly graduated from high school, he moved to Los Angeles, enrolled in film school, d began hosting at the Hollywood Improv. e told the L.A. Times, "I only wanted to e a comedian. Everything I've done happened ecause I couldn't be a great comedian." early two decades after arriving in southern California, his *40-Year-Old Virgin* grossed $177 million. Twenty years of emceeing, scriptwriting, punchup, failed pilots, successful pilots, pitching, rewriting, and producing led to a one-man zeitgeist-shaper.

Apatow was known to a lot of comics as "that kid who emceed at the Improv" ... until he became a multimillionaire.

All about the reps

It is not unusual to hear comics tell other comedians how to approach writing. However, with rare exceptions, those who comment on the work ethic of others tend to be unnecessarily harsh and disparaging about the comic who is perceived as less prolific. It's a weird sort of posturing—we're not talking about bench presses here ... it's art.

> Number one, I'm a free-speech militant and therefore want to defend the right of every American to tell offensive jokes in the worst possible taste. Satire is absolutely crucial to democracy.

Camille Paglia

HOW MUCH TO WRITE?

Five new minutes a week is viewed as virtuous. It doesn't matter if it isn't very funny—it's about appearing industrious and productive. Comics need to be seen as "writing machines," and anything less is slovenly, unprofessional. Novelists and painters don't have this pressure and are often referred to admiringly as "prolific," but the real reverence is reserved for writers like Joseph Heller, who wrote three novels in his life. Painters are permitted to take time creating masterpieces—no such luxury for the jokesmith …

Find a method and a level of proficiency that works for you. And always stay open to new methods.

Regenerate/discard?

Crowds want comics to do new material every time. For someone just starting out, it's better to find a method that works and develop it, rather than worrying about pleasing an imagined following. Build an act and refine it. Don't worry about rebuilding it according to some arbitrary timetable. Otherwise, build an act, use it for a while, burn it, then start over.

Clattering keyboards

Find the method that works for you. You can bump along at a snail's pace for ages, then one day decide to "go for it." Comics who say they write new material daily are probably fabricating (if they do, most of it will suck big time and be unusable). They say they must write two hours each day—meaning they're far more disciplined and willing to make bigger sacrifices. Listen to their material next time onstage. Hear the keyboard clatter as one "disciplined" joke after another is spewed out, often the product of writing exercises designed to conquer writer's block!

For how long?

You write like crazy in your first year or two, then you slow to a trickle, then it's periods of great productivity alternating with creative droughts. There's even a hackneyed saying: "You write your first half-hour in your first year" ... But is that half-hour any good? Some is, some isn't. Material changes, as do you. Some jokes survive, while most wither away because they aren't appropriate. Others cease to elicit laughs anymore! You massage them, you change the joke order, but nothing! So you write new jokes, but you hang onto the old ones just in case …

Louis C.K. (left, here starring with Jennifer Garner in *The Invention of Lying*, 2009) is regarded as a prolific comedian. He works as a writer, standup comedian, actor, producer, and director.

ENDLESS STREAM

Some comedians have to produce copious amounts of material on a daily or near-daily basis—staffers on late-night television talk shows, for example. Though they may produce mountains of material, no one expects it all to be high quality, and often there's a staff of writers engaged to do so. The best and most suitable material is chosen from that day's or week's output. The rest is discarded or held in reserve.

> "Yes. My mentor was Sophie Tucker who, in her day, was considered 'naughty' ... She caught me, or her writer saw my show and told her I did her 'Life Begins At Forty' song at my piano bar, and she asked me to have lunch at her hotel. She asked me why would I ever do that song when I was 24 years old? She also told me 'to be honest with my audiences as they will know if you're lying, because audiences are smarter than you think they are and they'll catch you on it every time.' They are ... and they'll catch you on it every time.
>
> Rusty Warren

WHAT IF I DON'T SAVE THE WORLD?

Comics are comics—period—and no one delivery method is more virtuous than another, so long as the end result is laughter. But some folks go one or two steps further and dismiss entire comedy subcategories of standup as being unworthy. According to these arbiters of "worth," anyone who uses a guitar in his or her act is hopelessly gauche, and someone speaking with a Southern accent (or another manner of speaking peculiar to a region) is branded a "goober comic," or "Newfie comic," or "Geordie comic," incapable of crafting an act that's little more than pandering to the baser instincts of a comedy club crowd. Does the comic use props? The critics would say that a prop comic should try to write jokes instead of relying on visual aids. An impressionist? Heaven forbid! Mimicry, don't we all agree, is for children or the feeble-minded—right? And on, and on, the critics go ...

Honesty!

Originality is always key. What we must also prize is—for lack of a better word—honesty. If a comedian approaches the task of making a roomful of people laugh with simplicity and genuineness, there should be no cause for complaint. Even if this genuineness is faked (and this is not as much of a contradiction as you might imagine), it's still a good thing. Little else matters outside of originality and honesty—seriously.

In a world dominated by political correctness, Sarah Silverman has been decidedly "incorrect" as often as possible.

Of course, it's always possible to work on two tracks: clean and noncontroversial for one performance, down and dirty for another.

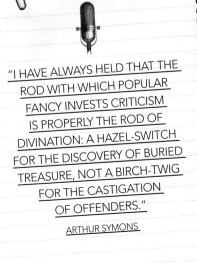

"I HAVE ALWAYS HELD THAT THE ROD WITH WHICH POPULAR FANCY INVESTS CRITICISM IS PROPERLY THE ROD OF DIVINATION: A HAZEL-SWITCH FOR THE DISCOVERY OF BURIED TREASURE, NOT A BIRCH-TWIG FOR THE CASTIGATION OF OFFENDERS."

ARTHUR SYMONS

P.O.V.

A point of view develops over time. Finding your basic sense of humor—and, if your goal is to be a standup comic, becoming calm onstage and developing performance skills—should be your primary objective early on. Pay attention to the things that amuse you. At the beginning, humorists might think they are obliged to "talk about what they know"—a nugget of advice given in comedy classes or books purporting to teach the secrets of humor writing. However, what if "what they know" isn't particularly funny? What if an accountant finds humor, not in numbers and actuarial tables, but in the antics of his pet ferret or in today's news?

Don't be afraid to be honest. Don't be afraid to lie through your teeth. So long as it's funny, they won't care.

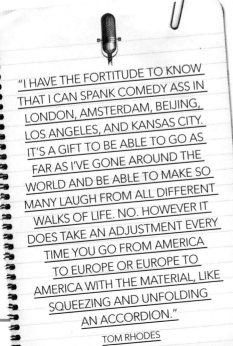

"I HAVE THE FORTITUDE TO KNOW THAT I CAN SPANK COMEDY ASS IN LONDON, AMSTERDAM, BEIJING, LOS ANGELES, AND KANSAS CITY. IT'S A GIFT TO BE ABLE TO GO AS FAR AS I'VE GONE AROUND THE WORLD AND BE ABLE TO MAKE SO MANY LAUGH FROM ALL DIFFERENT WALKS OF LIFE. NO. HOWEVER IT DOES TAKE AN ADJUSTMENT EVERY TIME YOU GO FROM AMERICA TO EUROPE OR EUROPE TO AMERICA WITH THE MATERIAL, LIKE SQUEEZING AND UNFOLDING AN ACCORDION."

TOM RHODES

Get an angle

Beginner comedians should lock into what they think is funny and trust that they've either focused on comedy territory that no one else has happened upon before, or that they can work that territory in a way that hasn't been worked before. In this way, they can talk about what they know … and talk about what they know to be funny.

Clean or dirty?

It's difficult to work clean or dirty. Why? Because it's difficult to be funny. How we approach comedy with regard to clean or dirty doesn't make it harder or easier, and there seems to be an awful lot of (unnecessary) controversy over this simple matter. One faction insists on linking "clean" and "clever," implying that a dirty comic is utterly incapable of being clever. Exceptions are made. Dispensation is granted to a select few—Richard Pryor or Lenny Bruce or Chris Rock— but they simultaneously imply that the only way clean comics can overcome the restrictions of working clean is by being clever, which means, by implication, that "dirty" comics aren't bound by such restrictions and are seldom clever. None of this is true, of course.

American comedians Fred Willard and Larry Miller have ties that go way back!

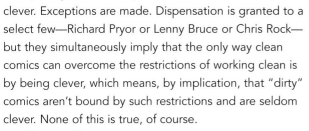

Comedians, actors, musicians, painters—and a lot of people disagree with me on this—but the first and only thing we should all do is entertain … I think there is great honor, passion, and light in entertaining people.

Larry Miller

> For a new comic, besides being a slave for the headliner, it is very important to keep writing and writing. As you grow as a comic you will find what you like talking about, and the garbage you have written in the beginning wil most likely get dropped, bit by bit.
>
> Rich V

ARE THERE LIMITS?

Short answer: No. Nothing is off-limits … but only if you're willing to own the joke, and it's funny. Long answer: If you're going to joke about subjects that are "beyond the pale," find ways to explain, and/or justification for the ultimate punch line. If you want to tackle subjects or scenarios that are obviously shocking, or that will most likely offend the sensibilities of a significant majority of an audience, realize that such an undertaking requires a great deal of care. It's specialist stuff, like being on the bomb squad. There will be many times when you're misunderstood, and not everyone is up to the challenge. Of course, it's attractive. It's tempting because there are no restrictions, so it's natural to want to broach territory that so many faint-hearted humorists have not dared venture into.

Brave heart

Some comedians start out as "sick" or "twisted" or "gross-out" comics, but learn very quickly that it hampers progress. Most beginner comedians lack the skill to write and perform disturbing material well enough to overcome an audience's revulsion. There's enough to deal with early on without having to deal with visceral and violent audience reactions to a joke that is (at least on its surface) "wrong." Be prepared for the worst, but by all means give it a go. Should the material evoke less than satisfactory responses, consider putting the material away and revisiting it at a later date, when your skills are up to selling it better.

The French comedian Michel Coluche (better known as Coluche) was famous for his irreverent sense of humor. He became one of the first major French comedians to regularly use profanities as a source of humor on French television, and was sacked from two radio stations due to this.

Delicate matters

Beginning comics find it hard to wring laughter from matters that are highly personal or tragic, or that play on the audience's emotions. It can be done, and the results can be satisfying for both audience member and performer, but in the early days—when sets are often five minutes long and/or in a comedy club setting—it's exceedingly difficult to deal with pity, sorrow, suffering, or grief.

COMEDY ABOUT RACE

American comedian Bill Burr does the near-impossible—he's a white comic whose standup deals with issues of race. That's quite a feat in these politically correct times.

CONTEXT ISN'T EVERYTHING, BUT IT IS SOMETHING

Comics can go too far. They will say things—in a specific place, on a specific occasion— that provoke people to observe they were inappropriate. This causes others to defend the comic in question, saying that others have no right to condemn them and that it infringes on their freedom of artistic expression. We're all for freedom of speech, but there are times when such comments from comedians might be regarded as inappropriate. And free speech or artistic expression need not be irreparably damaged— in fact, when it comes to performance, recognizing social conventions and observing some obvious boundaries actually preserve freedoms down the line.

Self-censoring is sometimes necessary and doesn't mean the end of your integrity as an artist.

Obviously not

You cannot do comedy at the Holocaust Museum. Nor can you crack jokes on the rim of an actively erupting volcano or in the immediate aftermath of a five-car pileup. "Sure, they were jokes about the lava and the smell of antifreeze and six million dead Jews! But they were jokes—doesn't comedy provide its own context? They come with their own protective coating. No need to think about taking umbrage. The statements were intended as jokes; that inoculates them against any kind of sanction, right?" Nonsense. It isn't everything, but context does count. Our examples are contextually different from, say, a comedy club, and are nowhere near analogous, and we exaggerate to make a point, but awards banquets, talk-show monologues, or corporate events have their own set of norms calling for restrictions on language or subject matter. Context is vitally important to assessing the appropriateness of a joke.

"ANYTHING GOES"

Context is our friend—not just something that hems comedy in. It liberates
our performance. When you define what can't be said, where, and by whom, you
essentially leave the rest of it wide open. So long as there are venues and
situations where "anything goes" (and there are always plenty of these), freedom
of expression is not harmed by occasional incidents where a performer has gone
over the line.

> All we can do is say the things they always thought but couldn't verbalize. You can't make people from onstage. All we can do is let them know what they think is just as important as anybody else's opinion. Make them think they can think. Which they can. We can empower them but not change them. But our first responsibility is to make them laugh. That's our job. That's how we get hired back. Make 'em laugh first and fit the trenchant opinions inside the punch lines.

Will Durst

4
STANDUP PREPARATION

Standup comedy is a diverse and unpredictable business, so it will come as no surprise to hear that there's no set method for learning how to make people laugh. There are certainly a few informal "rules," but the very nature of a comedian is to be a rule-breaker. No one goes to college intent on becoming a comic and attaining a degree in Funny; it's a calling that's arrived at via an infinite number of paths. How you approach the task of making people laugh is up to you, and you alone, but there are some principles that apply to performing in traditional standup venues. While not hard and fast, taking note of them may make the experience of venturing onto the stage at these establishments seem a little less mysterious (or scary).

OPEN-MIC NIGHTS

First-time comics at open-mic nights usually do five-minute sets (though this varies between two minutes and ten). It may not seem like enough time to display comedy brilliance, but if things aren't going well, 300 seconds can seem like an eternity. This means around 10 to 20 punch lines, depending on delivery and writing style—one-liner comics have more jokes; storytellers have fewer.

At first, time may seem to stand still ... pretty soon, it might be perceived as whizzing by. Wear a watch.

Be warned!

Five minutes is the *maximum*. Nothing angers the open-mic community more than a newbie going too long (or "going over"). Plan on doing eight jokes rather than ten, but make sure these are the best you have. It's perfectly acceptable to make your maiden performance three minutes long: comedians—at any level—make more of an impression with three funny minutes than three funny ones followed by two awkward ones.

Logistics

Nerves will probably completely distort your sense of time, so determine beforehand where the signal—the "five-minute light"—will be located. Many clubs flash a light when one minute, or 30 seconds, remains. (Clarify the method used by the venue, as performance spaces do vary.) Glancing at your wristwatch while performing is a no-no—it'll make you look more amateurish.

Comedy idols

All comics have comedy idols. What makes these people so humorous—the material? The delivery? We all tend to want to emulate the people we admire so much, but that doesn't mean we'll be able to pull it off. A naturally high-energy person will do a poor job of copying the style of a low-key, taciturn comic, and the comic who made us guffaw when we were in fifth grade isn't necessarily the same one who makes us laugh at age 20. People change, tastes change.

Ellen DeGeneres is an American comedian whose style has been likened to Bob Newhart. She is known for her deadpan, rambling style of observational humor.

COLIN QUINN'S "LONG STORY SHORT"

Quinn uses rapid-fire delivery, sarcasm, throwaway lines, and strategically placed F-words to tell the history of the world in 75 minutes in his standup show. It's headline-length standup set in a fancy setting, and there are no tears or heavy messages. Adopting Brooklynese, a unique attitude, and a plethora of accents, he recounts swathes of history using modern-day analogies, depicting England as a spurned lover constantly pining for France, and likening the Catholic Church after the fall of Rome to warring rap producers. It's history lecture disguised as freewheeling rant—deceptively well-written and exquisitely constructed.

> Standup implies a sort of confrontation between the performer and the audience, so people walk into a comedy club already on the defensive. Also, there is the feeling that the standup comic must prove himself worthy of being on the stage.
>
> Rob Becker

WATCH COMEDY

You can learn so much from watching a comedian work a roomful of comedy fans. Even more can be achieved by observing them do three or four shows in the space of a weekend. People still think professional comics do a different act every time they're onstage—mind you, there are also wannabe comics who think this! Yes, each performance by a comedian will contain slight, subtle differences—a different crowd, venue, and showtime all contribute to making each show unique—but most comics must, by necessity, do essentially the same act, seeking always to create an illusion of spontaneity. Comics' acts change, but not from show to show.

Tommy Chong was, for many years, one-half of the comedy duo Cheech & Chong. They still perform together on occasion.

GOLDEN COMEDY

While it may be enchanting to imagine our comedy heroes spinning original comedy gold every time the curtains part, the fact is they rely on a core of material and experiences to get them through a performance. This revelation may shatter the hopes and fantasies of novice comedy fans everywhere, but observing and appreciating the consistency, precision, and economy of a well-honed comedy act can give great pleasure. Observing this skill set in action repeatedly helps you understand what you eventually wish to master.

Watch as many different kinds of comedy as you can. Explore your own feelings toward each.

Be yourself?

Professional comics often tell beginners to "be yourself," but it's hard to do this if you don't know who you are offstage. Quite often, beginning comics are so young—so lacking in a "self"—they have nothing to draw upon, so such advice is practically worthless. Such advice can also be dangerous. Let's say you take the advice and are roundly rejected by an audience, or two, or three, which often happens. If you are yourself up there—and you've felt the sting of rejection—you might start feeling negatively about yourself. All because you wanted to make a few strangers laugh! It might be better to be a version of yourself. An exaggerated you. Or be a little more gregarious, boastful, or vulgar. Eventually, the onstage and offstage self will converge, much to the delight of audiences (and dismay of your friends). At the core, there must always be you. This basic "you" must be present, as audiences can smell inauthenticity.

Comedians should do what comes naturally to them. I love swear words in jokes when they're effective. Sam Kinison and I were friends—we appeared on one of Rodney's HBO specials together—and we both always enjoyed each other's styles and watching each other work. It never felt right for me to swear on stage. I save that for my personal life.

Rita Rudner

> # I had my persona from the start: it is the default persona when one has no stage presence.
>
> Emo Phillips

APPEARANCE— ARE YOU "YOU"?

Feeling comfortable with your onstage apparel is important. It is a mistake to wear anything that's distracting, and always a good idea to cover up any naughty bits. If a comedian is conveying a particular message, why wear a T-shirt with a slogan that contradicts it? Besides, it makes it harder for the audience to concentrate on what's coming out of the comic's mouth, and it's just foolish! These aren't hard and fast rules: if a first-time female comedian wants to mount the stage with a revealing outfit, she should go for it, but it's just one more distraction getting in the way of the message.

A medium is the message

That said, a comic's clothing should match his or her persona. It might, in a subtle way, even reinforce whatever message is being conveyed. However, it is paramount that the comedian should be unselfconscious. So pay attention to the nonverbal message that's being sent via the attire, and take care not to wear anything that might distract from the main mission.

Robin Williams is known for his eccentric shirts and outfits, which complement his offbeat humor.

Do you normally wear a tie? If you're going to wear one while performing, it had better be for a good reason!

Suits you?

Not used to wearing a suit? Don't wear one. Not comfortable in provocative or revealing clothing? Cover up and wear something more respectable. If you suspect a pair of jeans is not very flattering, leave them in the closet—otherwise, you'll spend the entire evening wondering, "Do they think I look fat?" A middle-aged mom—with material to match—shouldn't dress like a 20-year-old college student, nor should a comic who jokes about being broke wear a Rolex, or a tuxedo-wearer tell gags about being a mechanic. Unless, of course, irony is the goal—in which case, it had better be crystal clear. Otherwise, prepare to perform in a giant puddle of cognitive dissonance.

COMIC ARRESTED FOR OBSCENITY

You're thinking Lenny Bruce, right? Well, in 1960, eight years before Bruce was popped in San Francisco, Belle Barth was busted for naughty language. Her scrape with the law apparently didn't affect her in the same way it affected Bruce—seven years later, her album *If I Embarrass You, Tell Your Friends* sold one million copies!

"A COMIC PERSONA IS VERY IMPORTANT. IT'S HOW THE AUDIENCE IDENTIFIES WITH YOU. IT'S PART OF WHAT MAKES THAT SPECIAL CONNECTION. I WOULD HAVE EVEN MORE PERSONAE, BUT, SO FAR, THE MEDICATION IS PREVENTING THAT."

CHARLES VIRACOLA

MEMORIZE OR CHEAT SHEET?

When just starting out, memorization is the comic's best friend. Remembering tons of material is a necessary skill for comedy, and the sooner the training starts, the better. Seasoned comics are often seen consulting cheat sheets or cue cards during their sets. They are professionals. They've earned the right to "cheat."

Stand up straight ... unless your "character" slouches. Look up and out ... unless your "character" stares at the floor. You get the idea.

Or ...

The long answer is this: Pros have long ago ceased appearing nervous, and have a high comfort level and stage command. Open-mic comics do not have this, and sneaking an occasional look at a list marks them out as rank beginners. No such association is made in the mind of the audience if a pro does this, though. Maybe that's unfair, but it's the way it is.

Rehearse

Unlike actors, comic actors, comedy teams, and, yes, even improv troupes, standup comics don't need to rehearse—they do it in front of a crowd. This has its good and bad points. Bad: We fail in public more often than other entertainers do. Good: We get an immediate sense of what is and isn't working.

Dave Gorman, a British standup, believes it's impossible to rehearse standup: "You can't stand on an empty stage running through it; it's not a script that you learn, because the timing depends on the audience. The words are your tune and the audience is your instrument. You can't rehearse without your instrument—that makes no sense."

Lose the hairbrush

These can both help to calm you before going onstage. A comic can rehearse a set, in the privacy of a bedroom, while talking into a hairbrush … which unfortunately makes the live performance sound exactly like that! In other words, nothing substitutes for getting out in front of a roomful of living, breathing people in a club or similar venue.

"DEAL WITH SUBJECTS THAT NO ONE ELSE IS TALKING ABOUT AND DON'T FORGET TO SAY, 'GOOD EVENING, LADIES AND GENTLEMEN, MY NAME IS SO AND SO.' JOHNNY CARSON HOSTED *THE TONIGHT SHOW* FOR 30 YEARS AND EVERY NIGHT THE FIRST THING OUT OF HIS MOUTH WAS, 'GOOD EVENING, LADIES AND GENTLEMEN, MY NAME IS JOHNNY CARSON.' IF [HE] COULD SHOW THAT KIND OF HUMILITY, SO CAN A YOUNG UNKNOWN."

KIP ADDOTTA

FRANK FAY

American actor and one of the first modern standup comics, Frank Fay was cited by both Bob Hope and Jack Benny as a major influence. Born in 1891, his tempestuous marriage to actress Barbara Stanwyck was said to have been the model for the couple depicted in Academy Award-nominated *A Star is Born*. Fay is often thought to be a bridge between the vaudeville comics of old and the 1930s and 1940s comics dominating radio who later influenced television and live performance.

> Sometimes I have to do a joke 25 times before it starts working. I know I should give up around the 15th time, but I don't. In my regular set I have jokes that have *never* worked and I still keep trying. I think it's called chasing the dragon.
>
> Bonnie McFarlane

CLASSES

Classes or workshops are tremendously helpful for people who thrive in a group atmosphere, as some folks need other people's advice or support to work up the nerve to try comedy for the first time. Generally, however, comedy attracts the lone wolf—someone who wants to prepare and perform without any outside influence.

Good idea?

A class can give the aspiring comic a month or two of relatively painless comedy trial and error in a safe (and comparatively judgment-free) environment. Along the way, some handy stage techniques might seep in, or a handful of bad habits might be eliminated quickly. These habits may have lingered much longer, otherwise, being nearly impossible to detect and/or eliminate.

Trying material out

Once you've made up your mind to do it, it's advisable to only do material on an audience. An exception: A beginner who is taking a class might be instructed to try out material on classmates. Aside from that, trying it out on co-workers or strangers—in the office, in an elevator, at a lunch counter—is utterly pointless, because if they don't laugh, you'll lose confidence in the joke. And if they do laugh—but a real audience doesn't react in the same way—this can be disorienting and disconcerting. In other words, doing material in front of anyone other than a real audience is flawed, if not pretty worthless.

CHECK OUT THE STAGE

Nearly all comics, when they first test the comedy waters, have a fear of choking—a total inability to speak and perform. So, before giving comedy a try, watch a few professional shows and as many open-mic nights as you can. Quite often, this fear is merely a lack of knowledge or a fear of the unknown. Become familiar with the pitfalls, eliminate the variables, and fear will diminish! Before the show—with the permission of the club's owner—mount the stage, with the lights on, and get a feel of what it's like to be up there. First-timers often cite those blazing lights as the thing that stuns them most when they first step onstage. The deer-in-headlights effect has stunned more than one open-mic-er into catatonia, but if all else fails, try a few drinks!

There's no shame in taking a class or joining in a workshop ... or reading a book. Some folks need a conventional "push" to take the plunge.

FRIENDS OR STRANGERS?

Some folks feel comfortable doing comedy in front of people they know, but performing to strangers is often easier, and less disconcerting. Some seasoned standups still don't like to perform for friends or family. They regard it as their job— and who wants loved ones hanging around at work? They may have no problem doing standup in front of hundreds of strangers, but will be very aware of anyone in the audience they (even vaguely) know.

Call yourself a friend!

Because comics often present a skewed version of themselves onstage, they're not eager to reveal that side to friends and loved ones. Some friends might be supportive of the standup adventure, while others may be envious or hostile. Ascertain which friend is which before you send out the invitations! Some clubs require open-mic participants to bring friends (at least, paying customers) in exchange for stage time, making it difficult for comedians who wish to pursue the comedy dream in anonymity.

Do you need alcohol to summon the courage to perform? Do you need a lot of it? Perhaps comedy is not for you.

WHAT ARE FRIENDS FOR?

After a bomb, pals can boost morale … or can intensify feelings of embarrassment. An audience packed with friends might also give comics an overgenerous, if not warped, response. The last thing rookie comics want is "help"—they desire a genuine response from a roomful of strangers.

GEORGE CARLIN IN A SUIT?

George Carlin's "Seven Dirty Words" routine was central to a U.S. Supreme Court decision to regulate the airwaves when it came to foul language. His long hair, relaxed, conversational delivery, and use of "forbidden" words made him the quintessential counterculture comedian ... but he wasn't always the freewheeling comic that generations came to know and love. George Carlin wore a suit and tie up until at least 1967, and achieved success doing so (it was practically mandatory at the time for a male performer to wear a suit and tie when on network television). It was only later that he shucked the tie, initially in favor of a turtleneck, eventually ditching the suit in favor of more casual dress—jeans, plus sweatshirt or V-neck sweater. It's illuminating to note Carlin's sartorial progression as his onstage and television persona evolved (his material, delivery, and subject matter changed along with his clothing).

What you wear can be a joke. Intentionally or unintentionally. It's up to you. Experiment.

> I believe that standup is my favorite activity, and unless I lose interest or am blacklisted, I would like to do it forever. I really love it, except when I hate it.
>
> Andy Kindler

KILLING AND BOMBING

We can't guarantee you will ever kill, but you will bomb ... eventually. It all comes down to how you deal with the bombs. You don't require an outsized ego to be a comedian—quite the opposite. Don't take them personally, nor the kills. You can't do 14 shows a week if you're feeding an ego the size of Mars. It doesn't work that way.

Complacency isn't desirable. But neither is constant, churning dissatisfaction. Try to strike a balance.

THE "BIG THREE"

Like George Carlin (see page 93), Lenny Bruce sported a suit and tie in his early days, but he also had an act that went along with the outfit. His seminal performances in New York (and on television talent shows) were rather conventional: he did impressions—albeit offbeat ones—and was not, at least initially, considered someone who would change the world of comedy forever. His metamorphosis came about when he worked incessantly in the strip clubs of the San Fernando Valley. The "big three"—appearance, persona, material—are key, but you may not immediately figure out their correct combination. You need to find out what makes you comfortable, and your persona needs time to emerge.

"I DID STANDUP COMEDY FOR 18 YEARS. TEN OF THOSE YEARS WERE SPENT LEARNING, FOUR YEARS WERE SPENT REFINING, AND FOUR WERE SPENT IN WILD SUCCESS. MY MOST PERSISTENT MEMORY OF STANDUP IS OF MY MOUTH BEING IN THE PRESENT AND MY MIND BEING IN THE FUTURE: THE MOUTH SPEAKING THE LINE, THE BODY DELIVERING THE GESTURE, WHILE THE MIND LOOKS BACK, OBSERVING, ANALYZING, JUDGING, WORRYING, AND THEN DECIDING WHEN AND WHAT TO SAY NEXT. ENJOYMENT WHILE PERFORMING WA[S] RARE—ENJOYMENT WOULD HAVE BEEN AN INDULGENT LOSS OF FOCU[S] THAT COMEDY CANNOT AFFORD."

STEVE MARTIN

Moping or coping?

After smoking a room, do comedians have to raise their fists triumphantly? Is there a touchdown dance? Chest-thumping, along with sloppy kisses for unsuspecting bystanders? No. The demeanor is more placid. The same goes for a bomb. Moping? Snapping at well-meaning colleagues or clueless fans? No. Then begins a calculation of the days/hours/minutes to the next show, out of a need to erase any memory of the previous kill and prepare for the next performance. Yes, the just-completed show needs assessing, but the postmortem doesn't involve calculating the extent of crowd adulation—more a determination to replace any bad memories with positive ones. Modulating the highs and lows enables comedians to go show after show and deliver consistently good performances. It's a coping mechanism.

Some comedians describe performing as an out-of-body experience. Or they'll profess to be able to think of many disparate things at the same time, all while doing their act.

COMEDY MENTORS

Comedians do not need mentors. Being all-in-one writers/producers/directors, comedians are self-contained, but mentors can eliminate a lot of trial and error, and are invaluable. They might pass down some of their wisdom, if you seem particularly eager to learn. A comedian with a year's more experience than you still has more knowledge, so don't instantly seek out the advice of headliners.

STORIES TO TELL

You can get a ton of information just by listening to comedians' tales. They love to recount stories to other comics, and you can learn about life on the road, how to deal with hecklers, where to get work. Comedy mentors might take a special interest in your career, helping you to gain valuable stage time or introducing you to important contacts. Don't be a pest—be eager without getting annoying.

Teasing, ribbing, ball-busting

New comics may be totally unprepared for the offstage jousting with fellow comics. Comedians are merciless when razzing other comics—it's rarely done with malice, but is almost always brutal. Green rooms or comedy club bars are not politically correct zones. Comics are expected to give as good as they get, and take great pride in topping one another, but they also take great delight in being topped, and nobody laughs harder than a group of comics. If you're

Funny People, directed by Judd Apatow, 2009, starring Adam Sandler, Leslie Mann, and Seth Rogen. This movie focuses on the life of standup comedian George Simmons (Adam Sandler) who, after finding out about a life crisis, becomes a mentor to young standup Ira Wright (Seth Rogen).

thin-skinned or not comfortable in such a raucous environment, find another art form to pursue. Try a string quartet or tumbling troupe—they tend to be harmonious.

Contests

Clubs often use contests as promotional tools, sponsoring a Funniest Teacher or Funniest Reporter contest, for example. The atmosphere is generally upbeat, and they're a good way to get started. They also enable clubs to audition talent, and comics get to meet other comedians. Contest crowds are especially supportive of new comics; because prizes and crowd favorites are awarded, they get caught up in the thrill of the competition. Events advertised specifically for inexperienced comics are popular, because expectations are much lower. Beginner comics can also learn how to perform in a high-pressure situation—and a contest victory looks good on the résumé.

Am I an alternative comic? Well, I try to be funny, period, so if you tell me it's an 'alternative club' I'll give you alternative. Physical? I'll give you physical. Clever? Intellectual? I'll do that, too. I like a good challenge. Does a mountain climber just climb one mountain? Bring it on baby! I'll try it all!

Harland Williams

10 NEWBIE ERRORS

1. Staring at floor

Looking down is a sign of insecurity, giving the impression that you don't have confidence in either yourself or your joke— or both. If you're too nervous to make eye contact with the audience, look above them.

2. Not removing mic stand

Some comics choose to leave the microphone in the stand while performing. If you do remove it, take the mic stand and either put it behind you or off to the side. Standing or pacing behind a mic stand makes you look like you're not in control.

Keep the mic in the mic stand ... unless you like to take it out. But bear in mind that once you take it out, you'd better know how to hold it, use it, and put it back in.

3. Hands

Inexplicable gestures or playing with one's hair signify nervousness. Hands with minds of their own should be placed in pockets.

4. Saying "Um …"

Never say "Um," "So," or "You know," after a punch line or before. Combining all three—"Um, so, you know"—is far, far worse. Be concise.

5. Stepping on laughs

If the crowd is laughing, let them. Don't start your next joke before the previous joke's laughter has died down.

6. Not playing to entire crowd

While out of nervousness or a desire to look at friends, comics often look just left or just right. Looking all around pulls the crowd into your performance.

7. Playing with mic cord

The mic cord is not a lasso. Leave it alone—unless it's a physical hazard that must be removed.

8. Not memorizing act

It's a comedy act, not a soliloquy. Remembering a few minutes of jokes isn't that difficult. Reading from a piece of paper, or hesitating in the middle of a setup, throws your timing off.

9. Acting like the headliner

There's a fine line between confidence and cockiness. It takes a degree of hubris to go onstage initially, but temper this with some humility, especially if you are a newbie.

10. Attempting crowd work

There's already enough to focus on—jokes, lights, time, crowd. Why add another element by engaging the audience in banter? Time for this later.

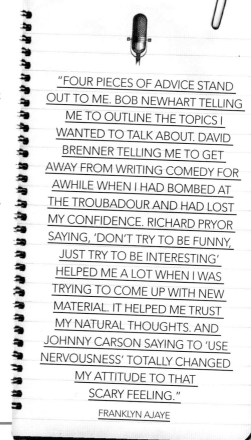

"FOUR PIECES OF ADVICE STAND OUT TO ME. BOB NEWHART TELLING ME TO OUTLINE THE TOPICS I WANTED TO TALK ABOUT. DAVID BRENNER TELLING ME TO GET AWAY FROM WRITING COMEDY FOR AWHILE WHEN I HAD BOMBED AT THE TROUBADOUR AND HAD LOST MY CONFIDENCE. RICHARD PRYOR SAYING, 'DON'T TRY TO BE FUNNY, JUST TRY TO BE INTERESTING' HELPED ME A LOT WHEN I WAS TRYING TO COME UP WITH NEW MATERIAL. IT HELPED ME TRUST MY NATURAL THOUGHTS. AND JOHNNY CARSON SAYING TO 'USE NERVOUSNESS' TOTALLY CHANGED MY ATTITUDE TO THAT SCARY FEELING."

FRANKLYN AJAYE

5
STANDUP PERFORMING

Surely you've heard the expression "Comedy is better than sex."
It's a part of the standup culture, but is not fair to comedy … or
lovemaking. Certainly, performing can be as pleasurable as sex—
perhaps even as disappointing. Standup comedy often has to be
performed on command, even if a comic is not in the mood to
do so. Talk to enough comics and you'll encounter frequent
references to a sort of mental orgasm that can occur while
performing. It's that brief, and all-too-rare, moment between the
words and the laughter, when your body and brain know
absolutely that something great is about to happen. Not unlike
what a legendary home-run hitter feels as soon as his bat makes
contact with the ball: he doesn't have to watch the ball leave the
stadium, because he knows where it's going.

HECKLERS

Heckling is probably the novice comic's top fear, edging out bombing or choking. While frowned upon, it's not exactly a capital offense—some venues immediately eject hecklers, while others merely keep a tight rein, only throwing them out when they become disruptive. The fear is understandable: the comic goes onstage with a batch of jokes and a clear idea of how to deliver them, when suddenly a hostile voice from the darkness issues a challenge.

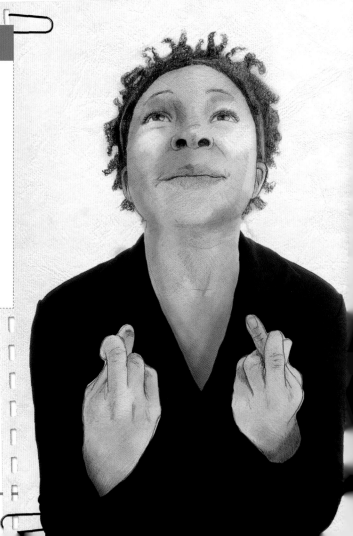

POWER STRUGGLE

Heckling is about power—the comedian has it and the heckler seeks to remove it—but hecklers, like dogs, can smell fear. Though tricky, the best tactic is to feign indifference. Remain calm, but you must respond. The retort itself is important, as is its mode of delivery. Attitude matters as much as content.

Eliminate the variables. Try to depend as little as possible on luck. Be prepared.

Show us your wares

Female comedians should prepare for the occasional sexual heckle, the most popular being "Show us your tits!" If they had a nickel for every time they heard the phrase, they could all pay for a really good boob job. Ho ho! The key to handling Show-Us-Your-Tits Guy: maintain control, and (as with most hecklers) you get only one chance. Put him in his place without insulting every male in the universe, which is tricky, but if done correctly the other men feel superior, the women feel vindicated, and Show-Us-Your-Tits Guy feels like a puppy who's just peed on an expensive rug. See right for some examples. The method you choose depends on your mood. Formulate your own responses.

"S.U.Y.T." COMEBACKS

DEFLECTION
Male heckler: Show us your tits!
Female comic: Dad, is that you?

SELF-DEPRECATION
Male heckler: Show us your tits!
Female comic: Sir, it appears you have bigger tits than I do.

VICIOUS AND CRUEL
Male heckler: Show us your tits!
Female comic: Show us your penis. It will definitely get a bigger laugh.

> don't think anyone ever gets over the surprise of how different one audience's reaction is from another … On your bad show, I found it useful to say to myself mentally, 'What a dimwit, stupid bunch of assholes you are!' I said it once aloud in San Francisco and it did not win them over but it made me feel marvelous. Today, of course, I'd be shot.
>
> Dick Cavett

HECKLER TYPES

Hecklers come in many shapes and sizes, and if you do standup long enough you'll encounter them all ... sometimes on just one tour. Here is the quintessential heckler compendium—the Standup Comic's Ten Least Wanted List. Some easily fit into more than one category, and if you ever encounter someone that fits into every slot, please alert the bouncers and have the evil specimen tossed out on its insecure and intoxicated little butt!

1. The power-hungry heckler

This pathetic little heckler deeply resents the fact that the comic has more power than he or she. A power-hungry heckler deals with this impotence and resentment by yelling, "Say something funny!"—even when the rest of the crowd is laughing. This type of heckler is the most common, and is usually more annoying than dangerous.

2. The heckler with bad timing

In a perfect world, a heckler would at least have the decency to heckle after the punch line and before the next joke begins.

The heckler with bad timing yells out during your setup, during the punch line, or between the setup and the punch line, quite often eliminating any chance of the joke getting a laugh. Since timing is everything in comedy, hecklers like this are particularly offensive.

3. The loud, drunk, female heckler

There is nothing more nightmarish than the loud, drunk, female heckler. Male comics find her difficult to deal with because society frowns upon a man who is mean to a

> Not that many clubs supported me early on. My first few years of touring rode on the fact that I could always find a new club I hadn't been to to make an impression.
>
> Mitch Hedber

woman—even a drunk, obnoxious one—as do female comics, for exactly the same reason. It's a no-win situation for either gender, which at best must be handled deftly. To make matters worse, loud, drunk female hecklers tend to complain to the management after they've been removed from the premises. They also write letters to the club management once they've sobered up.

This would be Heckler Type #3. Approach with extreme caution!

"THE RULE ABOUT HECKLING IS THIS: YOU FIRE AT A COP, GET READY TO DIE. YELLING 'YOU'RE NOT FUNNY' AT A COMIC IS FIRING WITH AN AK. HURT YOUR FEELINGS? TOUGH. ANYTHING GOES FOR HECKLERS, INCLUDING EXCESSIVE FORCE. I LAY MYSELF BARE UP HERE, AT MY MOST VULNERABLE YOU SHOOT ME IN THE CHEST; I WILL KILL YOU IF I CAN. YOU KNOW WHY [MICHAEL] RICHARDS LOOKED SO SHELL-SHOCKED AT HIS OWN OUTBURST? BECAUSE HE'S NOT A RACIST, HE WAS SIMPLY IN THE ZONE. COMEDY CLUBS ARE LIKE INDIAN RESERVATIONS. THEY ARE THEIR OWN COUNTRY. I DON'T THINK HE SHOULD HAVE APOLOGIZED. YOU PAY YOUR MONEY AND YOU TAKE YOUR CHANCES, STEP RIGHT UP."

ELAYNE BOOSLER

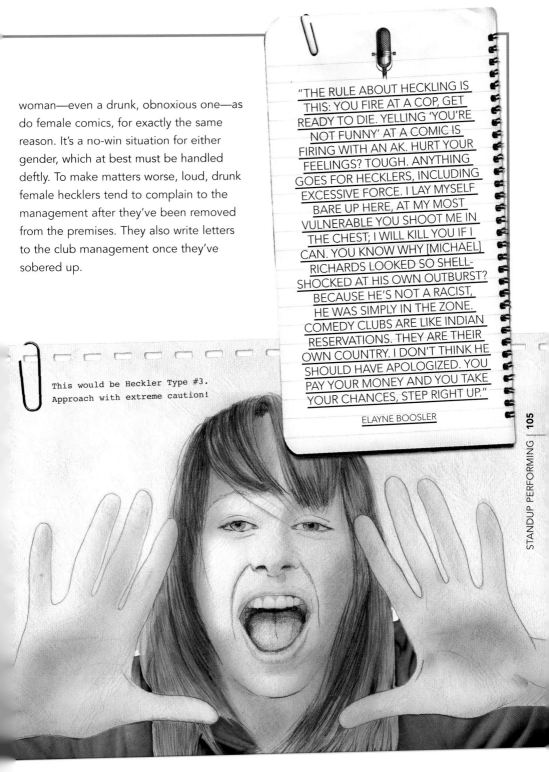

4. The nonsequitur heckler

These hecklers yell out nonsense—say, the word "turtle"—for no apparent reason. Very confusing. And especially confounding when the comedian has made no reference to turtles, or any other marine life. Dealing with nonsequitur hecklers can often result in an easy laugh, since they do most of the work for you.

5. The heckler no one else can hear

This disruptive sort sits in the front row and talks loud enough to be audible only to the comedian and the heckler's annoyed tablemates. Irritatingly, the comic can't easily retaliate, because most of the audience has no idea anything's amiss. They never stop— because they're nearly unstoppable. This heckler doesn't ruin your show, just your life for the duration of it. Let's hope a Category #3 heckler is waiting for a fist fight in the parking lot!

6. The heckler who won't repeat the heckle

An audience member heckles, the rest of the crowd laughs, but the comic hasn't heard. In an effort to wrest control of the situation, the comic says, "What did you say?" but is ignored, and has no comeback because he or she didn't hear the initial heckle. This is terrorism by tongue, by a cowardly heckler who is willing to bask in the glory of the laugh but won't risk being topped— which is pathetic.

Forewarned is forearmed. "The Heckler No One Else Can Hear" will unnerve you if you aren't ready for him.

7. The heckler who beats you to the punch line

Occasionally, audience members can see exactly where your joke is heading. Very, very occasionally, one of them pipes up with your punch line … before you do. Like a small child, this heckler has been incited to do something socially unacceptable. Yes, it is wrong, but you cannot really get mad. In the race to the punch line, the comedian's timing can be thrown. Take pity, or take it out on the heckler—it's up to you.

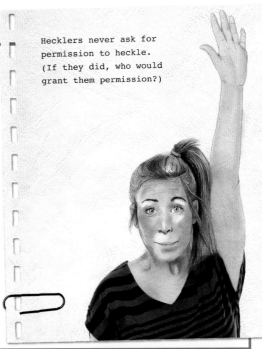

Hecklers never ask for permission to heckle. (If they did, who would grant them permission?)

> Well I have this thing built into my contract that the club has to put up a sign that says my act 'contains the strongest language and material content imaginable,' but, believe it or not, I still get complaints. People want you to be what they want you to be, ya know? If they see you on TV and that's what they like, they want you to be EXACTLY like that when they see you live. And if you're not, some of them get upset.

Joe Rogan

Kathy Griffin is a rare specimen: a storyteller. Her tales of celebrity encounters fulfill the public's need to "dish" on a grand scale.

8. The heckler who makes up his or her own punch line

The performer gets a laugh, as does the heckler. The performer gets another laugh; so does the heckler. So it goes for the entire show. The heckler's laughs will be bigger than yours if he or she is with a large group, and you'd best leave the heckler alone and allow him or her a moment in the sun if the yelling isn't too intrusive. When he or she starts jumping on your punch lines, that's game over. The balance of power has shifted unfavorably. Declare war.

9. The heckler who gets personal

Harassing or disconcerting isn't enough for some hecklers. They aim to hurt the comic deeply and personally, for no apparent reason. Recognize it when it rears its ugly head—sometimes it manifests itself as insulting remarks about physical appearance or cutting barbs about female relatives. The attacked performer is advised to breathe deeply before forming a response—dealing with a heckler requires equanimity, not white-hot rage, as showing fear signals that the heckler has won and the all-important power balance might shift. Via some sort of cosmic code of justice, this heckler is giving the comedian permission to get personal in return, so feel free to attack the female relatives, choice of clothing, or mental acuity.

10. The heckler who gives opinions

The comedian does a joke and this charmer says, "That was a good one." Another is met with "I didn't like that much." One more joke and "Now, that was funny!" After a few beers, this heckler is doing rim shots. If this heckler also happens to fall into Category #5, this can make for a long evening. Deal with this kind of interruption head-on and with logic. Any response needs to convey "I appreciate your assessment, but you are merely echoing the sentiments of those who are trying to enjoy the show. I suggest that you henceforth keep your running commentary to yourself." Or, failing that, "Shut the **** up."

Common denominator

Some hecklers may be hard to identify or categorize. But there is undoubtedly one thing they have in common. After the show, they will come up to you and say, "I helped the show!" No … you did *not*.

In earlier times, audiences were less refined, more hostile, and thought nothing of tossing objects at the performers!

> That's actually one of the keys to my act, my act is so completely and totally uncensored that the only way I could really pull it off is if I treat the audience like they're my best friends and I talk to them completely honestly. People for the most part can smell lies.
>
> Joe Rogan

POST-PERFORMANCE POSTMORTEM

You may be tempted to bask in the glory of the kill and soak up adulation from your peers after a successful performance. After a poor show, you might feel more inclined to skulk away and try to forget about it—perhaps drown your sorrows with some whiskey ... or a good quantity of chocolate milk.

Questions, questions

What is most helpful, in terms of your progress, is a quick, honest assessment of what occurred. Did you achieve everything you wanted to? Did it go as planned? Did you improvise something that worked well? If something went badly, why, and can you avoid it in the future? Ask these questions immediately after the set; otherwise, after the adrenaline wears off, it will be much harder to recall the adjustments you made or your brilliant spur-of-the-moment observations.

Norman Wisdom pictured in his dressing room at the Palace Theatre, Manchester, after appearing in *The Smell of the Grease Paint, The Roar of the Crowd*, September 1964.

NOW OR NEVER

Time is of the essence because of what's known as state-dependent memory, which you may remember from college psychology. Scientists drugged up a bunch of rats and had them run around a maze multiple times until they learned it, and when the rats came down from the drugs they couldn't recall the maze very well, until they were drugged up again. Put another way, your ability to remember things is affected by your environment, intoxication level, or emotional state at the time.

Comics under the spotlight—with adrenaline, endorphins, or alcohol coursing through their veins—are in a radically different state than when they exit the stage. Waiting too long to recall any changes or new stuff might be very difficult. Although the redrugged rats were able to find their way around the maze (see box, left), it's not wise to depend on getting "performer's high" again to recall the changes you made to your set. Better to find a quiet corner for a few minutes, jot down a few observations in your notebook, then join one's friends for some strutting and puffery. Or buy a small, digital audio recorder.

You may not always be happy with a performance ... but there's always another one around the corner.

Comedy is ... really not like any other art form in that it's very specialized and varied in its content, but generic in its title. You would never go to a club just to see 'live music': you would go to a jazz club to see jazz, a blues club to see blues, etc. But when you go to see 'standup comedy,' if you don't know the performers' material, you really don't have any idea what you're gonna get. You might get Barry Manilow, or you might get Rage Against the Machine.

Joe Rogan

> In Detroit, the water company was working on the sewers and cut the power by accident. It happened two hours before the show on opening night. No lights, no sound, no plumbing! I did the show in the lobby. Had people light some candles and sit on the floor. It worked wonderfully.
>
> Bob Dubac

RECORDING

Recording a set on video and watching it later is probably the most important thing a new comic can do to assess progress and make improvements. Chances are that adrenaline will either keep you from remembering clearly just what transpired onstage or give you a false sense of what actually happened.

Listening to the set afterward is a good way of memorizing and editing.

Keep notes

This isn't to say that you shouldn't make an instant, pencil-and-paper assessment. In fact, the first crucial minutes after a set should be spent alone, recording anything pertinent you observed that will improve your future performances. This avoids the inevitable self-recriminations when—in the absence of a recorder—you cannot remember that improvised line or inspired twist on a well-received joke.

Video quirks

Videotaping isn't nearly as important for a more seasoned performer, but early on, watching yourself on videotape is a quick way to eliminate bad habits. Though cringe-inducing, viewing videotape is crucial. Beginners may not realize they deliver punch lines straight into the floor (the number one rookie mistake) or repeatedly play with a lock of their hair—there's no limit to the variety of distracting mannerisms novice jokers seem to come up with. Poker players call these "tells"; audience members view them as annoying. There's no need to hire a camera crew to record your open-mic performance or to spend thousands of dollars on a high-def camera. Often a smartphone will suffice—so long as you can get a visual record of what you've done, you can analyze it and gather enough data to make changes next time.

TREAT YOURSELF

A small audio recorder should be the comic's first gift. Modern digital recorders can be slipped into a pocket before a performance, or placed discreetly on a stool onstage, or even placed on a speaker or unoccupied table at the back of the room. This also helps to record spontaneous remarks made during your set. Jokes can be written or improved onstage; but, if you forget what you said, they could be lost forever. A digital backup can augment the "acoustic" version scratched out with pencil and paper. Better yet, use videotape.

Nearly everything you do physically must have a reason. Otherwise, it is probably distracting.

STAGE TIME

If comedy muscles are not exercised, they atrophy. Superstars of comedy aren't made by occasional monthly appearances. Comedy isn't just about timing; it's about time. It takes years to become a competent standup comic and a lot of shows to get good. A weekly show is the bare minimum, twice a week is better, but five times weekly is better still.

Spread the word

People who live in big cities are lucky enough to be able to do several open mics in one night. But even the smallest towns usually have more than one weekly venue, and if they don't, start one up! The other open micers will know where you can perform and when, so talk to them. Tell them you are seeking stage time—share information and you will get information in return.

Gotham Comedy Club, on 23rd St. between 7th Ave. and 8th Ave, is the epicenter of New York City's comedy scene. It's been the backdrop for numerous network and cable television tapings.

MONOLOGUE/DIALOGUE

Never, never ask your audience a question—unless you are prepared for a response. If you frame a statement as a question, they will see this as being invited into your monologue and at that moment it becomes a dialogue. The simple act of asking, "So, where are the single ladies in the audience?" could start an interaction—or, worse, heckling—which a beginning comic is unprepared to handle.

Crowd work

Interacting with an audience member—
"going into the crowd"—takes bravery,
quick wit, and confidence. Comics should
never use crowd work just to kill time, as
it will look like that's what they're doing.
Talking to individual audience members
is a skill developed over time, if at
all. Crowd work—the moment when
comedians talk to a member of the
audience and improvise a response—
takes a tremendous amount of confidence
to abandon the prepared remarks and
work "without a script."

> FOR ME, SHOWTIME IS
> SHOWTIME—I FOCUS
> ALL DAY ON IT—IT'S NO
> PARTY FOR ME. I WANT
> TO GIVE THE AUDIENCE
> ALL MY GUTS AND
> ONCE IT'S OVER, GET
> INTO BED ASAP.
>
> RICHARD LEWIS

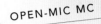

OPEN-MIC MC

Emceeing is a good
way to practice
crowd work, and
doing it at an open-
mic show is especially
effective. There are so many
opportunities to mount the
stage anew, and interact
with audience members in
short bursts.

Writing a joke has never embarrassed me.
But having to stand onstage and look people
in the eye who are offended by what you are
saying can be pretty humiliating.

Bonnie McFarlane

NEW MATERIAL

It is vital to develop a stage persona and get some experience—learn how to make a joke work, how to assemble a set. If you do new material each time onstage, these skills will probably never be acquired. There is room, however, for new material. Always do at least one new bit onstage each time: a topical joke (one with a short "shelf life"), a tagline, a tweak, or a brand-new two-minute section. Hone the old stuff while getting comfortable with something new.

The joke that got away is the one you didn't write down immediately. Carry a pad, a mini audio recorder ... or napkins. Write it down.

"ALTERNATIVE" VS. "ALTERNATIVE"

In the U.S. a gang of standups came along (mainly in New York City and Los Angeles clubs) who sought to differentiate their particular brand from most other comedy being practiced in mainstream clubs. Their standup was often performed in unconventional venues, frequently using offbeat presentation and dealing with atypical subjects. Of course, these comics had always existed, and many had worked in the comedy clubs for years, but more and more comedians flocked to New York and Los Angeles, and it became harder to stand out—so these comedians latched onto the "alternative" label as a brand. In the U.K., "alternative" defines a wave of comedians gaining notoriety in the early 1980s, arising in reaction to, and to distinguish themselves from, the old-guard comedians populating British entertainment—particularly television, and mainly men—who honed their acts in working men's clubs and music halls. Like their American counterparts, the "alternatives" used absurdity, political astuteness, outrageousness, and even a willingness to offend. This set them apart from their comedy forebears, whose methods and sensibilities were similar to those of American vaudeville or Catskills comedians.

Suckitude

The expectation of suck is both distressing and oddly comforting to beginners. They aren't expected to kill—usually, they're expected to eat it—and this "nothing-to-lose" mindset lends itself to experimentation, exploration, and prodigious output. There's plenty of latitude for suckitude; but, as the bombs thin out and the kill takes over, this reduces. As competence increases, tolerance for incompetence decreases.

Ballsy or cautious?

Getting through the first few intimidating shows is a hurdle. Some people stand onstage for minutes at a time and polish a work in progress, risking stretches of silence and maybe even incurring the audience's wrath. Others are more cautious and analytical. Find out what works best for you, and don't be dictated to.

> Audiences are my best friends ... You never tire of talking with your best friends.
>
> Bob Hope

> I recently found a notebook I thought was lost and there was my old act, not written out but with abbreviations ('Chinese–German food,' 'Wedding gifts,' etc.) and in one margin I had noted: 'Woody said, "Great joke, Cavett."' It reminded me of the sweat and labor of getting a second show, something I'd not foreseen … What struck me was that virtually all of it would work today. I'm trying manfully not to say, 'Funny is funny,' but I'm afraid it's true. I might update the act some by uttering 'motherfucker' every few minutes. Years have passed since I have set foot in a comedy club. If the comic is doing badly it's painful, and if the comic is doing brilliantly, it's extremely painful.

Dick Cavett

HONING OLD MATERIAL

Never throw away old jokes. Keep every napkin, piece of paper, computer file, and audio recording you have ... forever! Jokes that don't work in your first year may kill 10 years later. Sometimes it's a matter of discovering how to do the joke better, or where it belongs in your act; or you may not have the confidence to give the joke what it needs. Occasionally, a comic suddenly sees a connection between two jokes—jokes that heretofore have never worked but, in combination, do. For this reason and others, no joke should be discarded. Review them sporadically. Try one out and, if the joke doesn't work, put it away again and look at it another time.

Left to right: Director Brad Bird, Patton Oswalt, and producer Brad Lewis, during the production of *Ratatouille*.

PATTON OSWALT AND DAVID CROSS

Cross and Oswalt are frequently cited as quintessential alternative comedians, and represented the movement in the 1990s. In countless interviews and articles, they defined what it was to be alternative and fearlessly expressed their distaste for mainstream comics, fans, and clubs. But, as with all revolutions, the revolutionaries inevitably become mainstream, and inevitably parlayed their rebelliousness into starring roles in nonalternative projects. Oswalt achieved success in Disney/Pixar's *Ratatouille* and as a recurring character on CBS Television's *King of Queens*. While Cross initially achieved notoriety as a star of the seminal alt-comedy sketch series *Mr. Show*, he moved to conventional network television with recurring roles in Fox's *Arrested Development* and the quickly canceled *Running Wilde*, plus a high-profile appearance in blockbuster children's movie *Alvin and the Chipmunks*, and *Chipmunks II* and *III*—the three movies could easily gross $1 billion. Both comics continue to do edgy, alternative comedy in their live presentations.

ORDER OF PERFORMANCE

First, you try to develop a 15-minute act. Then you get some work.

Opener or MC

The opener or master of ceremonies (compère in the U.K.) does 15 minutes. Sometimes he or she does 10 minutes upfront—"starting the show"—then five more minutes before bringing on the headliner. This spot is the second hardest position on the bill, so why this difficult task is left to the most inexperienced performer is a mystery. (Some cities do insist on having the headliner act as the MC—they're the main attraction and the other comics on the bill are the "special guests.") Emceeing is the best way to gain the necessary experience to move up the comedy ladder. A conscientious MC will work far more often than one who doesn't take the job seriously.

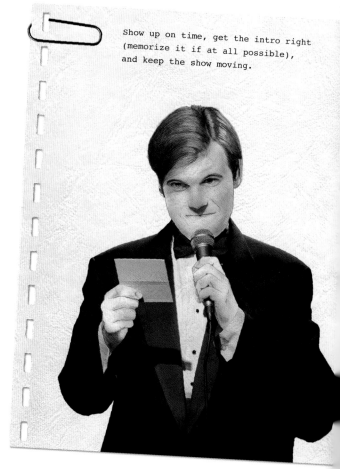

Show up on time, get the intro right (memorize it if at all possible), and keep the show moving.

Middle

The middle or feature spot is undoubtedly the best place to be on the show. The audience has already been warmed up by the MC, there's no pressure to close the show, and the crowd is usually at its energy peak. A 20- to 30-minute set is usually required.

TOE THE LINE

You'll be responsible for warming up the crowd, introducing the other acts, making announcements, and saying goodbye. You are the glue holding the show together. An MC should never go over time or do anything that sets a strange tone for the rest of the evening. Some clubs won't even allow an MC to curse—and for good reason: clean headliners don't want crowds becoming accustomed to obscenities, while dirty headliners don't want all the shock value squandered by the first person on the bill. Try to memorize introductions and announcements (it's far more professional). Be nice to the audience, stick to time, and suppress your ego—let others get more applause. Do all this correctly, and you'll have the freedom to hone your jokes and break in new material. Don't take on the job unless you're sure you can do at least 15 minutes—without laughs.

WARNING!

Don't assume (erroneously) that, just because you have tremendous sets as a middle act, you are automatically headliner material. After all, you are performing under near-ideal conditions. It's foolish to mistake your rollicking success in the middle position as *prima facie* evidence that you are ready to headline. As we shall see, the headliner spot is a bit trickier than it looks.

> An opening act is expected to prepare the audience for the headliner. To hand the audience to the headliner on a silver platter.
>
> Kip Addotta

> "Dom Irrera once described me as 'The best car comic working.' I was funny until we got to the club. Then I became totally preoccupied with doing a half-hour because I only had 20 minutes. I would lie to people and tell them I was on stage for a half-hour. The only reason I worked was because I owned a car."
>
> Jonathan Katz

KEEP GOING

Pacing is crucial, as is the ending of the set. It's tough to maintain attention through bathroom breaks and multiple drinks orders. The closing spot brings all manner of special considerations with it, and requires a broad skill set. Quite understandably, the headliner also makes the most money and receives the most glory ... which is why everybody wants to headline.

Closer

Closers (headliners) are expected to perform for at least 45 (even 60) minutes. The show's success rests squarely on the headliner's shoulders. Even if the crowd loves the MC and middle act, if the headliner bombs, they feel they've seen a bad show. There is a vast difference between the presentation of the opening act and that of the closing act, which is keenly felt by those called upon to close a show.

Theo Maasen is a Dutch comedian who has changed the face of Dutch standup, by moving away from traditional cabaret-style comedy and pushing boundaries of good taste with his irreverent humor.

OUTSIDE THE COMFORT ZONE

However long you've been doing comedy, it is highly advisable to take on a task that you are not 100 percent sure you can master, or one you're not sure will turn out well. A (noncomedy) observer might think that merely going up at a comedy club—with a healthy crowd, on a weekend evening—is a challenge. But choosing an exercise that's far outside one's comfort zone, while possibly fraught with "danger," has huge benefits. It rearranges the brain, makes you think differently, and bolsters confidence in areas where there might still be insecurity. Failing might initially engender feelings of inadequacy or doubt, make you work harder, or help you accept your limitations, but it also allows you to focus on your strengths. It's nearly always a winning proposition long-term, even though at the time it feels like a train wreck.

Discomfiting

Adventures outside the comfort zone can prevent a comic from becoming complacent. The opposite of complacency is "anxious," but anxiety gets you places and can be a great motivator. Most comics swing from anxiety to complacency, with varying frequency and amplitude. Most good comics are acutely aware when they're operating from uncertainty and when from contentment; they take on the challenges knowing (or intuiting) that to do so will undoubtedly work to their advantage.

NOT ALL ADVICE IS GOOD

Beginning comics know how their presentation should go, how it should be perceived. Changes will undoubtedly need to be made as the vision progresses. Some of these are informed by the comics' inner voice, while others are suggested by "real" people—club owners, audience members, other comics, or bartenders.

"Hey! I got a joke you can use in your act!" Uh ... no you don't. Be polite. Be firm, but polite.

WHO KNOWS BEST?

Are outsiders better placed to suggest tweaks? Examine the motives of those suggesting changes in tone, a different approach, or alternative punch line. Before it even comes your way, investigate how you feel about advice. It often causes inner conflict, so maybe thank the advice-givers and then ignore them.

Aesthetic choice or subconscious tic?

Comics often have an array of nervous mannerisms, many exaggerated during a performance, and there'll be no shortage of well-meaning others seeking to remove such tics. Examine these quirks and determine which (if any) could be genuine, interesting, or even useful in creating an onstage persona. Some of these affectations may be distracting, others endearing or, at the very least, benign. They could help differentiate you from the rest of the pack.

Comedians have a tremendous amount of freedom to craft an act and a persona to their exact specifications.

Writer/director/ producer

As the writers, producers, and directors of their stage performances, standups are unique among performers. It's both liberating and, in rare cases, paralyzing. Standups are also free to change the tone, direction, message, and medium of their performances—mid-career or mid-performance!

STANDUP PERFORMING | **125**

"INCIDENTALLY, I WAS ALWAYS BEST IN A CLUB WHEN HECKLED. BUT I LEARNED QUICKLY THAT IT'S HARD TO GET BACK INTO YOUR ACT. THE THRILL OF TOPPING SOME BOOB IN THE AUDIENCE MAKES RETURNING TO THE PREPARED STUFF SEEM ALL WRONG. IT TAKES SOME EXPERIENCE TO LEARN TO FINESSE THAT."

DICK CAVETT

LONG LINE OF ONE-LINERS

Jimmy Carr is the latest in a line of deadpan, one-liner comics. Comedians trading in simple, original, setup/punch line jokes have been around since the beginning of standup time. Carr, Stephen Wright, and Mitch Hedberg can trace their lineage back to Henny Youngman, who affected a deadpan delivery and played the violin while telling dozens of one-liners in quick succession. "King of the One-Liners," he started his career working in a print shop, selling joke cards containing many of the succinct gags he'd later use in his act. All four of the above-named comedians achieve laughs via a similar method, and are noted for a warped worldview. But, due to their distinct personas and divergent deliveries, they're radically different.

6
VARIETY ACTS

Centuries ago in Italy, actors performed plays in open-air settings in a form of theater called *commedia dell'arte*. Performances were free, and the troupes would travel from town to town, perform, and then pass the hat around. These performers are considered the first professional actors, and the peculiarities of this 16th-century variation on theater are notable because in every one of the *commedia dell'arte* companies there were three main roles—servant, master, and lover. "Comedy" referred to any play or dramatic work that was light, humorous, or satirical in tone—that is, anything that wasn't tragedy—so if it didn't end with characters weeping over a bleeding body, it was a comedy. The three characters (plus slight variations) were standard in every production. The servant was a goofball, usually from the country, often shiftless, sometimes athletic or acrobatic, and became popular among those who gathered to watch the plays. He became known eventually as Harlequin, and nearly all comedians can be traced back to him.

CLOWNING

Most world cultures have needed buffoons, fools, and clowns to lighten things up. In Native American tribes, they were considered able to cure diseases, and in royal courts jesters provided levity and, according to some experts, influenced important decisions. One of them, Archibald Armstrong, entertained—and had some sway with—King James I of England.

Clowns were around for centuries before anyone thought to put one in a circus.

Female clowns are a relatively modern development. Clowning was dominated, until very recently, by men.

Little guy, Big Man

It is undecided whether jokers had any actual juice with emperors, kings, or elders, but one thing is certain—they've been around for a very long time. At the heart of their work, the clown, the jester, the satirist, and the political comic all represent the little guy struggling to triumph, even in little ways, over The Man. Put another way, comedians—no matter what tricks, gimmicks, makeup, costuming, and language (or silence) they employ—deal with the human condition. And in doing so they elicit laughs.

BILL IRWIN

Irwin is a "new vaudeville" clown, which is one of the four or five major categories of clowns. They do not typically wear makeup, they often work alone, and they interact with the audience, breaking the "fourth wall." Irwin is also an accomplished actor, having won a Tony Award in 2005 for Best Actor in a Play (*Who's Afraid of Virginia Woolf?*). Irwin started out as a whiteface clown—another of the main clown categories, and the oldest of them all.

MUMP & SMOOT

This Canadian clown twosome (Michael Kennard and John Turner) are often referred to as "The Clowns of Horror." They work mostly in theaters throughout North America. The logo at the top of their web site drips blood—unlike most clowns, Mump & Smoot are not intended for children. One critic likened their work to that of Samuel Beckett.

Creepy clowns

In modern times there's been a clown backlash—pop culture is rife with references to "creepy" or "scary" clowns. (An irrational fear of clowns is known as coulrophobia.) When the details of serial killer John Wayne Gacy were made known in 1978 and 1979, and gory newspaper accounts were accompanied by a photo of him in full clown regalia as his alter ego, Pogo the Clown, clown-fearers felt vindicated. Horror novelist Stephen King wrote a book, *It*, about a clown that murdered children.

Clown culture

Methods, costumes, and makeup have been surprisingly impervious to change over the years. Clowns have a strong sense of tradition, which is passed on from generation to generation, and even have "clown colleges" where aspiring clowns go to learn or refine makeup methods, pantomime, prop comedy, and other tricks of the trade. They have codes of conduct and strict rules regarding dress, performance, and when and where to remove their makeup.

You know ... clowns can get away with murder.

John Wayne Gacy to surveillance officers before his arrest

Modern clowns

Modern clowns barely look different from their predecessors of 50, 100, or even 200 years ago. There are variations among clowns, of course, but the basic formula is unchanged. American clowns are closely associated with the circus. But clowns are everywhere— private parties, in theaters, at carnivals and street fairs, and on television—and a large a part of Europe's cultural landscape.

Clownie roomies

Many different kinds of performers can trace their methods, directly or indirectly, back to clowning. Penn Jillette, Bill Irwin, and Michael Davis all attended clown college, and their current acts are, to varying degrees, influenced by their experiences there. Each in his own way is still a clown, though no one would mistake them for clowns as we understand the word.

One is a mime, the other's about as loud as one can be. They dazzle with illusions and magic, while simultaneously debunking the art form.

THE GOOD NEWS? I'M GOING INTO MEDICINE ...

In July 2009, the University of Haifa announced that it were establishing a program in Medical Clowning. This dual-major degree focuses on areas related to therapy, as well as theatrical skills necessary for clowning. Don't laugh! A recent report showed that the success of in-vitro fertilization procedures was greater among women who were entertained by a professional "medical clown" right after the embryos were implanted.

JOSEPH GRIMALDI

Grimaldi is recognized as the first whiteface clown, and he was so associated with clowning that clowns are often referred to as "Joeys." Born in England in 1778, Grimaldi used pantomime and was a major innovator. He served as the bridge between ancient and modern clowning.

ALBERT FRATELLINI

Albert Fratellini is said to have popularized the use of the red nose. Clowns had red noses before him, but never the bulbous costume-party fixture that we know and love today. Moscow-born Fratellini is also said to have redefined the auguste clown, another major clown category famous for tricks, tripping, falling, and other slapstick.

MR J.S. GRIMALDI.
(as Scaramouche.)

"Grimaldi is dead and hath left no peer. We fear with him the spirit of pantomime has disappeared." The *Illustrated London News* on Grimaldi's death.

RED SKELTON

Son of a clown, Skelton was successful in movies and radio before being lured to the small screen. One of his most famous characters, Freddie the Freeloader, was a silent clown who told a story through pantomime. Freddie was a so-called "tramp," a type of clown developed in 19th-century America and modeled after members of the itinerant subculture referred to as "hobos." He also gained a reputation as a fine artist, his paintings mainly depicting ... clowns.

Variety

If asked, people would describe a comedian as someone standing on a stage, alone, and evoking laughter using only words—a monologist. If you're intent on being a comedian, however, there are many other ways you can do so. Comedians through the ages have combined various specialized skills with standard monology to create a number of comedy genres.

MIME

Some performers combine comedic or clowning skills with silence—which makes them mime artists. "Mime" is short for "pantomime," the art of telling a story without using words, instead drawing on body movements, gestures, and facial expressions. If you're looking for suggestions on how to tackle comedy, the idea of someone getting laughs without even using words or sounds should pretty much shake you to your foundations. It tells you that you can do anything to get laughs ... including saying nothing.

Mr. Bean (played by Rowan Atkinson) is a British comedy character whose slapstick, naïve comedy antics (that never promise to save the world) are popular from England to Japan.

Mime vs. comedy vs. film

Not all mimes are funny. But there have been many comedians who use mime in order to create comedy. Rowan Atkinson, as the popular Mr. Bean character, uses elements of mime, and American television comedians Sid Caesar and Red Skelton frequently pantomimed sketches. Jerry Lewis was also well known for doing pieces that combined music and pantomime. Silent film stars Buster Keaton and Charlie Chaplin used mime in their movie performances (and were mimes who didn't seem to mind the technical limitations of a medium without dialogue).

French actor and comedian Dany Boon began his career dubbing cartoons and performing as a mime in the street. This background informs his physicality in acting and standup.

> They say pantomime's a lost art. It's never been a lost art and never will be, because it's too natural to do.
>
> Buster Keaton

> "Charlie's tramp was a bum with a bum's philosophy. Lovable as he was, he would steal if he got the chance. My little fellow was a working man and honest."
>
> Buster Keaton

Physical humor is often referred to as "clowning around," as demonstrated here by Buster Keaton and Thelma Todd in *Speak Easily* (1932).

How to tell?

There's a difference between a mime and a clown. Clowns usually focus on one character (which is usually reinforced via makeup and dress), whereas mimes use more subtle makeup and attire, and endeavor to represent many characters, not just one. There was a mime backlash in the 1980s, which saw mimes used (with alarming frequency) in television and movie scripts as punch lines—often violent ones. The mime backlash was concurrent with the clown backlash.

MIME BACKLASH

1991's *Scenes from a Mall*, starring Woody Allen and Bette Midler, was shot by director Paul Mazursky almost entirely in a shopping mall. Throughout the movie, the couple frequently encounters a mime (played by Bill Irwin in whiteface). Allen becomes increasingly annoyed as the mime insinuates himself into their conversations. Eventually, in a climactic scene, he punches him in the face. Some reviewers cited the scene as the best part of the movie.

BLUE MAN GROUP: CLOWNS IN "BLUEFACE"?

Three men, painted blue, combine props, music, lights, pyrotechnics, and multimedia in inventive ways to present a show on location in seven cities on three continents ... all without saying a word. Blue Man Group is hugely popular in Las Vegas and one good reason for this is that they don't speak. Sin City attracts visitors from around the globe, so not using speech is a very simple way for performers to get around the language barrier. It beats having to learn several languages, doesn't it?

Blue Man Group explores themes such as science and technology, information overload, and innocence.

JUGGLERS

Juggling is one of those specialized skills that can enhance a comedy act. Some jugglers seem to think that "comedy jugglers" aren't the most proficient jugglers, and that the juggling comes in second to the comedy. Perhaps such comparisons are pointless, because comedy juggling and juggling are two very separate things. Nevertheless, concentrating on jokes while keeping several objects up in the air at the same time can't be particularly easy!

Juggling history

What we know is that people have juggled for centuries. And at various times jugglers were enjoyed by regular folks in the street or lauded by the ruling class and by royalty. For a while, though, the rulers of the Ming Dynasty grew tired of jugglers and deemed them to be vulgar. During the Middle Ages, religious clerics (who called the shots) proclaimed jugglers to be off limits, claiming that they were amoral or maybe even witches.

Into the spotlight

It wasn't until the circus was invented (toward the end of the 18th century) that jugglers got a little respect. Philip Astley, the "father" of the circus, thought they fit right in. Jugglers also performed in music halls, vaudeville and burlesque theaters, and, of course, on the streets. But they fell on hard times when radio came along. Juggling, as you might imagine, doesn't make for great radio!

ORIGINAL COMEDIAN-JUGGLER?

Michael Davis claims to be the original comedian-juggler of the new vaudeville. And who are we to argue? He combined a wry delivery with pretty amazing juggling feats. He engaged the audience with his banter, and he brought a touch of the absurd to the ancient art. He appeared regularly theaters and on television.

Up in the air, On the air

Television breathed some life into the art of tossing and catching multiple objects. Variety shows often featured circus acts ... like jugglers. And, in the late 1960s and early 1970s, "new vaudeville" acts like The Flying Karamazov Brothers and Michael Davis gained popularity.

The appeal of balancing, tumbling, juggling, and other acts of physical prowess spans the globe and spans centuries.

WILLIAM CLAUDE DUKENFIELD A.K.A. W. C. FIELDS

W. C. Fields began his career in vaudeville as a tramp clown juggler. Initially, he didn't speak during his act, so that he could perform internationally. He started to tell jokes when performing for American audiences and eventually went on to develop the character that has become a comedy icon.

The word "juggling" derives from the Middle English *jogelen*, which means "to entertain by performing tricks."

COMIC MAGICIANS

Many comedians started out in show business as magicians. Whether as children or young adults, they took up magic, which gave them their first taste of performing. And through doing magic for crowds, large and small, they developed confidence onstage. Many subsequently abandoned the tricks and illusions and became straight monologists, but many did not. A number became comic magicians. Some comedians are actually very good magicians, other comics are deliberately bad magicians, while some are both.

Bad magickers

The most famous comics to employ the "bad magician" shtick are Carl Ballantine, Tommy Cooper, and The Amazing Johnathan. Ballantine became the first magician to headline in Las Vegas, and said that he became a comedian when he realized he could never be as good as the other magicians of his day. Cooper, a British prop comic/magician, always wore a red fez. He was a technically proficient magician and was held in high respect by his magician peers. Amazing Johnathan, the "Freddy Krueger of Comedy," has authored a book on magic and currently headlines in Las Vegas.

To be a successful "bad magician," you must first be a technically proficient (or "good magician").

PENN & TELLER

Penn Jillette and Teller (his name is legally "Teller," no first name) are accomplished magicians and illusionists, but they are also comedians. Their magic act, performed mainly at the Penn & Teller Theater at the Rio Hotel Casino in Las Vegas, seeks to entertain, amuse, and enlighten. Penn is the taller of the two. He is also the louder of the duo: Teller rarely (if ever) speaks, and chooses to use mime in the course of their performances.

TOMMY COOPER

British comic—magician Tommy Cooper is famous for his tricks that more often than not failed—to hilarious effect. He is also renowned for collapsing from a fatal heart attack during a performance on live television on April 15, 1984. Cooper, wearing his trademark red fez, is helped into his golden cloak by an assistant. Seconds later, he slowly falls to the floor, and eventually he slumps further down and then falls backward. Throughout his collapse, the audience continued to laugh, totally unaware of his plight. Attempts to revive him backstage were futile.

A statue of Tommy Cooper stands in his hometown of Caerphilly, Wales. (Photo at left is not the statue.)

MUSICAL ACTS

We're not talking musical comedy here. That's an entirely different animal—with vast casts, giant theaters, and choreography by the Lycra legful. What we're talking about here is the tight combination of music and comedy, more often than not involving a solo act or a duo (and, very rarely, three or more people—like, for instance, Corky & The Juice Pigs).

Mid-century comics, schooled in vaudeville, felt compelled to incorporate song and dance into their comedy routines.

Musocomedy? Comedomusic?

Mixing music with comedy has a long tradition. There have been countless comedy acts in vaudeville, burlesque, music halls, radio, television, movies, and recorded music that have utilized music, in one form or another, to one degree or another. Music has been used by comic performers who sing well, who sing poorly, or opt not to sing at all. Some musical comedy acts play an instrument—a number play very well; others, not well at all. (And there are also comics who deliberately play appallingly!)

I did it my way

Musical acts take many different approaches. Weird Al Yankovic does mostly song parodies. The Flight of the Conchords perform original compositions. Classically trained pianist Victor Borge ("The Clown Prince of Denmark") would mix wordplay with slapstick and the occasional serious number. Comedians such as Jack Benny or Henny Youngman used music only sparingly, as a counterpoint to the spoken humor, similar to the way music is used by contemporary comedian Zach Galifianakis.

> My live act, at its technical peak in 1976 through 1985, had nine audio cues and thirty minutes of rock 'n' roll and country music of which none was ever allowed on television.
>
> Gary Muledeer

TIM MINCHIN

Australian musical comedian Tim Minchin describes his act as "a funny cabaret act" that consists of songs at the piano interspersed with standup routines. With his heavy eyeliner, bare feet, and wild hair, Minchin is visually as well as aurally memorable, and exaggerates his hair and eyes in order for his facial expressions to be more noticeable. "I'm a good musician for a comedian and I'm a good comedian for a musician, but if I had to do any of them in isolation, I dunno." The subjects of his songs range from social satire to his failure to become a rock star.

Hans Teeuwen is a Dutch comedian and musician who has a brand of modernized cabaret-style comedy. His approach is physical, and he swaps between English- and Dutch-language performances.

THE BLUES BROTHERS

They debuted on *NBC's Saturday Night Live* in 1978 and went on to become a cultural phenomenon. Dan Aykroyd as Elwood Blues and John Belushi as Jake Blues fronted the blues revival band known as The Blues Brothers. Backed by solid musicians (like legendary Donald Dunn and Steve Cropper of Stax Records fame), the band sold millions of records and made two movies, *The Blues Brothers* (featuring Aretha Franklin, James Brown, and Ray Charles) and *Blues Brothers 2000*.

> But my method is I'm trying to find a really unique subject that's unique to me, or a personal thing that's happened to me. The more personal it is, the more unique it is, the more people will identify with it because you're emotionally attached to it. I don't talk about current events or politics or anything like that only because, well I don't like it. It doesn't appeal to me, but also when you make comedy records you want something that will stand the test of time that if somebody picked it up 20 years from now, they'd still laugh at it.

Rodney Carrington

PROP COMICS

If you use an object—be it a rubber chicken, a hat, or a telephone—in the service of getting a laugh, this is called prop comedy. The objects used can be everyday objects, used humorously, or the items themselves can be amusing. A comedian who engages in prop comedy—not surprisingly—is known as a prop comic. The term is sometimes used disapprovingly, as they are often (wrongly) frowned upon by other comedians.

Using a physical object to get your comedic point across is not as easy as it looks.

Winters witters

Occasionally, when Jonathan Winters appeared on a talk or variety show, the host would set aside a few minutes, during which he would hand the comedian random objects, prompting Winters to improvise miniature comedy routines based on each item. Winters is mostly known for his zany characters and surreal flights of fancy, but he is fondly remembered by many for doing what amounts to prop comedy.

The slapstick

Prop comedy was highly popular in the vaudeville era, and it has always been employed by clowns. Many clown routines utilize chairs or magic props or outsized objects. Indeed, an entire subgenre of comedy derives its name from an object—the slapstick—which was a paddle made from two pieces of wood, bound together at one end, which made a loud clapping noise. It was used in pantomime to strike a person but without causing injury, as well as in *commedia dell'arte*. Along with the whoopee cushion, it could just be the first prop.

Propping off?

Many comedians use one or two props here or there. Nowadays, however, it is rare for a comedian to build an act that is entirely, or predominantly, prop comedy. For one thing, there's the practical consideration—it's a logistical nightmare having to drag all that stuff around from venue to venue. For another, it's hard work having to keep all your props in decent working condition.

Gallagher Too (above) is Leo Gallagher's younger brother, Ron Gallagher. He was ordered by the courts to stop impersonating his older brother's seminal "Sledge-O-Matic" routine.

GALLAGHER

Leo Gallagher, known simply as "Gallagher," uses props in his act, most notably a giant sledgehammer, with which he smashes various fruits, vegetables, and other objects, much to the delight of his audiences. As well as using props, he is also a monologist who uses wordplay, social commentary, and political humor in his act. At the height of his popularity in the 1980s, he dressed like a mime, sporting a beret, a horizontal striped shirt, black pants, and suspenders.

"

Also, I just happened to take a Theatre of the Absurd course in college, and that's where it really started for me. It had this great little device, which is that when you perform absurd material, you can't really fail. No one can say, 'Hey, that wasn't absurd.' It gave me permission to try all the things I wanted to show people. It was inventions. It was bad magic tricks, weird concepts. Fortunately, the comedy boom was just getting going in Minneapolis. I started performing my junior year in college, then that whole senior year I did standup, and by the time I graduated, I was headlining.

Joel Hodgson

JOEL HODGSON

Hodgson created *Mystery Science Theater 3000*, after achieving fame as a comedian and appearing five times on *Late Night with David Letterman* and four times on *Saturday Night Live*. Hodgson was noted for designing inventive and bizarre props for use in his act. Three of those props—robots Tom Servo, Gypsy, and Crow T. Robot—became his *MST3K* co-stars.

"

CARROT TOP

"Carrot Top," a.k.a. Scott Thompson, is an American prop comedian, and has headlined the Atrium Showroom at the Luxor in Las Vegas for the past five years. Unlike most other prop comedians—who tend to use found objects as props—Carrot Top often fabricates bizarre props to serve as visual aids for his jokes, combining disparate items in incongruous ways to form three-dimensional visual gags. In addition to the props, his live show utilizes music, sound effects, photographs, lighting, and video along with straight standup comedy. Carrot Top could be described as a new vaudeville prop comic, owing to his outlandish stage name, his embrace of multimedia combined with modern standup comedy, and a propensity to engage the audience and frequently make self-referential commentary.

Carrot Top famously lost all of his props in a fire at a comedy club in Alabama.

IMPRESSIONISTS AND IMPERSONATORS

Impressionists are comedians who mimic the voice and (usually) mannerisms of famous people. Audiences are thrilled by a comic who can accurately approximate the speaking or singing voice of their favorite entertainers, politicians, or celebrities. The casts of countless sketch, variety, and television panel shows invariably contain one or two actors who are capable of "doing" the famous political figures of the day or who can serve as stand-ins for singers and pop stars.

SCTV

Particularly adept at mimicry were the cast of *SCTV*, the Canadian sketch comedy show from Toronto's Second City troupe. The versatility of Martin Short, John Candy, Andrea Martin, Joe Flaherty, and the rest of the crew, gave them tremendous license to create surreal scenarios that might include Orson Welles, Salvador Dali, Liza Minnelli, or Indira Gandhi.

Rory Bremner (here doing an impression of Tony Blair) is a British impressionist specializing in political caricatures.

Not the same

Standup comics who have featured impressions as some or all of their acts include Rich Little, Frank Gorshin, Marilyn Michaels, Fred Travelena, and Charlie Callas (all of whom were featured on Little's television show *The Kopycats*, which was filmed in England). David Frye perfected impressions of dozens of celebrities from movies, television, and politics, becoming particularly well known for his interpretation of President Richard Nixon. Many standup comics do one or two offbeat impressions in the course of their club acts, but that doesn't make them impressionists—impressionists are noted for doing many impressions well (or one impression exceedingly well).

VAUGHN MEADER

Vaughn Meader was a comedian who discovered he had a knack for imitating President John Kennedy. His album, *The First Family*, in which he and a cast of actors recreated fictional scenes from the White House, sold over seven million copies in a little over a year. (However, following the assassination of Kennedy, the sales plummeted, as did Meader's popularity.)

RONNIE ANCONA

Ronnie Ancona is a Scottish comedian, actor, author, and impressionist who won a 2003 British Comedy Award for Best TV Comedy Actress for her work in *Alistair McGowan's Big Impression*, a BBC1 show that featured the work of McGowan and Ancona, along with that of Jon Culshaw, Jan Ravens, and Steve Nallon.

"I THINK OF MYSELF AS AN ARTIST, AND IMPRESSIONISM IS WHAT I DO. I PAINT IN BROAD ENOUGH STROKES TO ESTABLISH A LIKENESS, THEN FILL IN FINER DETAILS, REAL AND IMAGINED THAT COLOR THE WAY I'D LIKE YOU TO SEE THE CHARACTER ... YOU KNOW, GIVE IT SOME ACCENT OR EXAGGERATION FOR COMIC EFFECT. IT'S MUCH MORE DELICIOUS FOR ME TO PUT A CHARACTER THROUGH A DISTORTION FILTER. THE MORE SUBTLE, THE BETTER. I'M NOT GOING FOR ANYTHING GROTESQUE, NECESSARILY ... I GO FOR 'SURREALITY.' IT'S A GOOD MIDDLE-GROUND PLACE TO BE THESE DAYS."

JIM MORRIS

When he died at age 72, Frank Gorshin was impersonating another comedian, George Burns, in the Tony-nominated play *Say Goodnight, Gracie.*

What a ruse!

One kind of impersonator essentially does an impression of someone who isn't well known. For example, someone could be hired to pretend to be the head of an organization dealing with insurance, and comes into a gathering of insurance professionals to speak to them. Only one or two people will in be on the gag; the rest of them believe that they're about to hear an expert, or an advocate, or perhaps even the CEO of their company. The impersonator starts out by speaking authoritatively on one or two topics that are familiar to the audience, but then goes off the rails and says outrageous things; perhaps even insults some of those present.

Who are ya?

Other impersonators seek to pass themselves off as famous people. These celebrity impersonators dress and behave just like famous entertainers or political figures. Some are silent—they're basically just props who pose for pictures at personal appearances or private parties or corporate gatherings—while others also speak or perform like the celebrities they impersonate. This sort of impersonator is mentioned here because they do occasionally impersonate comedians. In the U.S., Joan Rivers and Rodney Dangerfield were often recreated; in the U.K., there is a current trend offering so-called "tribute" shows seeking to reproduce the acts or sketches of British comedians such as Peter Kay or Eric Morecambe.

GOT WHAT IT TAKES?

Impersonation is a specialized skill and is not for the faint-hearted. It also requires improvisational skills, combined with an ability to absorb detail and information quickly. Once this information is absorbed, this has to be turned around, and crafted into a credible, if somewhat brief, presentation.

JAPANESE OBAMA IMPERSONATOR

Japanese comedian Nozomu Sato, 43, a comedian widely known as Notchi, started impersonating Barack Obama in early 2008, but is now Japan's only full-time Obama impersonator. When Obama was celebrating his election in November 2008 in Chicago's Grant Park, Nozomu and his wife were watching the event on television 6,000 miles away, full of excitement. Thanks to Barack Obama's election, Notchi is now enjoying an enormous boost to his 20-year career, despite being nine inches shorter and 44 pounds lighter than his muse.

VENTRILOQUISTS

Early ventriloquists were more concerned with demonstrating a skill than getting laughs. Ventriloquism was more about dazzling an audience by "throwing one's voice"—making a voice seem like it was coming from somewhere other than the performer's mouth. Emphasis was placed on not moving the lips.

RADIO VOICE-THROWING

Edgar Bergen was apparently the first to mix comedy and ventriloquism. He was certainly the most famous. Bergen performed in vaudeville, then segued into a long career on radio (who'd have thought ventriloquism would work on radio?). He also achieved success in movies and on television.

What Edgar Bergen lacked in technical skill, he more than made up for in charm and humor. And the "dummies" were pretty talented, too.

PAUL WINCHELL

No one incited more children to bug their parents for a dummy than Paul Winchell. His U.S. television show aired for three years in the mid-1960s, and his characters were sold through the Sears catalog. Winchell was also an inventor, with an interest in medicine. He developed several patents, including one for an artificial heart (with Dr. Henry Heimlich, inventor of the Heimlich Maneuver).

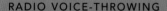

"S'AWRIGHT"

Spanish ventriloquist Wenceslao Moreno was more popularly known as "Señor Wences." He appeared frequently on *The Ed Sullivan Show* in the U.S. and was notable for his unorthodox creative choices and dazzling technical proficiency. During his act, he would engage in high-speed dialogue with Johnny (a face drawn on his hand) or Pedro (a rather macabre head in a box), and switch back quickly and effortlessly between his own voice and Johnny's falsetto, or between his voice and Pedro's guttural growl. His back-and-forth with Pedro popularized the catchphrase "S'awright."

Ventriloquists are part of a comedy team where only half the team is human!

Ventriloquism today

Ventriloquism remains popular, as evidenced by Terry Fator's victory in *America's Got Talent*. As part of the show's top prize, he received $1 million in cash and subsequently signed a contract at the Mirage Resort and Casino in Las Vegas. According to *Forbes* magazine, both Fator and fellow ventriloquist Jeff Dunham each make more than $20 million a year.

NO DUMMIES

They're not "dummies," they're "figures." Ventriloquists often conceive of a figure—a character they can build an act around—and then have one custom made. However, most aspiring ventriloquists lack the cash for this, and instead settle for an "entry-level" figure. These have rudimentary moving parts—a mouth that moves up and down, for instance, or, if they're lucky, movable eyebrows.

When I was doing the fairs and I was an unknown, they said, 'Oh, he's a ventriloquist, he must be a kids' performer,' so they would stick me over at the petting zoo. Now, when I started mixing impressions and ventriloquism, it was an interesting phenomenon because all of a sudden, I went from having 10 to 20 people at a show to filling up every single chair.

Terry Fator

> All we can do is say the things they always thought but couldn't verbalize. All we can do is let them know what they think is just as important as anybody else's opinion. Make them think they can think. Which they can. We can empower them but not change them. But our first responsibility is to make them laugh. That's our job. That's how we get hired back. Make me laugh first and fit the trenchant opinions inside the punch lines.
>
> Will Durst

POLITICAL COMEDIANS

The excesses of the ruling class provide much fodder for comedians. From Will Rogers to Mort Sahl to Jon Stewart to nightly monologues on late-night talk shows to television shows such as *That Was The Week That Was*, *Have I Got News for You*, or *Mock the Week*, comedians have performed the necessary task of giving voice to our frustrations with those who are spending our money and telling us what to do.

Political parody

Political satire has never been in short supply. It can be dispensed with a song ("Capitol Steps"), with puppets (*Spitting Image*), in a sketch (*Saturday Night Live*), or on a stage in a nightclub (Lenny

The "Rally to Restore Sanity and/or Fear" was a gathering that took place on October 30, 2010, organized by comedians Jon Stewart and Stephen Colbert. The demonstration drew over 200,000 people, and was a response to the growing prominence of Tea Party rallies in the U.S.

Bruce, Dennis Miller, Lewis Black, Stewart Lee). Unlike political protestors, satirists don't necessarily carry an agenda or try to influence their listeners' views. More frequently, their aim is just to entertain.

THE MOUSTACHE BROTHERS

On the other side of the planet, the Burmese comedy team with the zany title of The Moustache Brothers is mixing it up with its country's government. The comedy threesome are known for their "screwball comedy, classic Burmese dance, and sharply satirical criticism of the totalitarian Burmese military regime." However, the sharpness of their criticism managed to send two of the brothers to a labor camp for seven years in 1996. As a condition of their release, they are now not permitted to perform to anyone except foreigners and, even then, they can only do so inside the garage of their Mandalay house.

Some political comedians actually make concrete sacrifices for their art. Some even go to jail!

TAKING ON HUGO CHAVEZ

Political comics the world over make quite a show of "speaking truth to power," but few in the West are ever in any real danger of persecution for what they say or believe. This makes the antics of Venezuelan comedian Benjamin Rausseo pretty heroic. In 2006, Rausseo (also known as "El Conde del Guacharo,"—The Count of Guacharo) announced that he planned to run for president against Hugo Chavez. The Venezuelan president isn't known for being charitable toward his opponents. Another Venezuelan humorist, columnist, and comedian, Laureano Marquez, takes frequent satirical jabs at Chavez in a weekly newspaper column. He was recently presented with an International Press Freedom Award as one of the region's most courageous newspaper columnists. Marquez insists that he is an equal-opportunity offender. "Humor is almost always a reaction of the weak against the powerful," he says. His jibes have consequences—there have been calls by various government officials for his newspaper, *Tal Cual* (So What), to be "investigated," as it is suspected of plotting a coup against the president. Recently the television network that Marquez appeared on was denied a license.

"Political humor" deals specifically with politics, but can also explore social issues, popular culture, and economics.

CLOWNS AND COWBOYS

Dan Rice was an American clown—perhaps the most popular in the 19th century. He was also a political humorist and friend to prominent politicians Jefferson Davis and Abraham Lincoln. His clown costume was in a red, white, and blue American flag motif, and it is said that he was the model for Thomas Nast's illustration of Uncle Sam. His style is described as folksy, and not unlike that of Will Rogers, another folksy, aphoristic political humorist, who achieved international fame a quarter-century after Rice's death. Rogers appeared onstage in a cowboy outfit, twirling a lasso while delivering comedic monologues on the news of the day.

Bill Hicks has been the subject of documentaries, books, and retrospectives since his premature death in 1994. He described himself as "Chomsky with dick jokes."

CHARACTER COMEDIANS

What if you don't particularly feel like being yourself onstage, and if you'd prefer to be someone else—a character of your own invention? A wild exaggeration of yourself maybe, or someone who shares absolutely none of your traits?

It's her or me

Creating a character is an interesting way to approach comedy. Many iconic comedians mount the stage as someone entirely different from their real selves. Australian comedian Barry Humphries, for example, performs in the guise of Dame Edna Everage—a suburban housewife— who evolved into a multimedia dame starring in television and movies (and even writing an "autobiography").

The more famous Sacha Baron Cohen becomes, the harder it will be for him to fool people.

COMEDY JUMP-START

In 1959, Jack Paar invited actor-comedian-musician Cliff Arquette onto his popular late-night talk show. Arquette, who had all but dropped out of entertainment at the time, accepted, appearing on the program as folksy Charlie Weaver and reading a letter from back home in fictional Mt. Idy. Thus began a quarter-century of output that ranged from recording to writing, to acting, to, perhaps most famously, a regular resident of a square on the popular American game show *Hollywood Squares*.

ALI G, BORAT, BRUNO

Sacha Baron Cohen immerses himself in a character, then engages unsuspecting "marks" in conversations, adventures, and stunts. These "meetings" are then filmed and edited to tremendous comic effect for television and movies.

LARRY/DAN

Dan Whitney developed his Larry the Cable Guy into a smashing success. His catchphrase "Git 'er done!" has morphed into a brand unto itself. Whitney appears as the befuddled bumpkin in movies and on television, and has parlayed the popularity of the flannel-clad Everyman into a multimillion-dollar merchandising juggernaut.

"When I was being Ali G and Borat I was in character sometimes 14 hours a day and I came to love them, so admitting I am never going to play them again is quite a sad thing ... It is like saying goodbye to a loved one. It is hard, and the problem with success, although it's fantastic, is that every new person who sees the Borat movie is one less person I 'get' with Borat again, so it's a kind of self-defeating form, really ... It's upsetting, but the success has been great and better than anything I could have dreamed of.

Sacha Baron Cohen

7
SKETCH WRITING

What is sketch comedy and how does it differ from standup comedy or improvisational comedy? Sketch comedy is usually done with two or more people; it is usually planned out either in scenarios and beats, or totally scripted. Whereas standup comedy is usually one person getting up and telling jokes, or sharing observations and maybe stories, improvisational comedy is a group of two or more people playing make-believe for a period of time. Sketch comedy is a planned performance by multiple players. The domain of sketch comedy is the brief vignette that begins in a relatively truthful place and then begins to delve into the comedic by establishing a premise—an assertion or proposition that forms the basis of the sketch. The sketch writer has a theory that he or she believes to be funny and he or she is going to go about proving it by using comedic means. What's wonderful about sketch comedy is that it serves as a tool for social and political satire. You can make people laugh and maybe even make them think. For the comedian who prefers to work with others, who prefers to take an idea or concept he or she thinks is funny and craft a short play from it—a vignette—it is an ideal art form.

ALI REZA FARAHNAKIAN—THE EPIPHANY TO THE PROFESSION

I have been doing this for more than 20 years, but it began with an epiphany. One Christmas Eve, while back home from college watching television in my parents' living room, I felt lost as to what I was going to do with my life. While watching *Saturday Night Live*, a program that I had watched all my life and which had brought me such joy, I suddenly said to myself, "I will work on this show at some point in my life." And once the words had been uttered, the die had been cast. After the show was over that night, I went up to my room. I began to write down sketch ideas, and to put together what I would later learn was a running order—a list of sketches, in a particular order, that would obtain maximum force.

Ali Reza Farahnakian worked hard to make his dream of sketch writing a reality—and now teaches others how to do the same. In this chapter, he shares his journey and insights.

Learning the technicalities

Ideas were coming to me now. They had always been there, mind you, as I had grown up in a small town and we played a lot of make believe, imaginary play, telling stories. I enjoyed short stories—the *Twilight Zone* TV series— and shorter-format mediums, and it was all making sense. Sketch comedy appealed to me: I had watched as much of it as I could when growing up. I began taping *Saturday Night Live* on a VCR (video cassette recorder) and transcribing the words to see what they looked like on paper. I dissected the show.

SNL BREAKDOWN

Saturday Night Live has an opening scene—what I would later find out is called the "cold open"—then a monologue, maybe a commercial parody and scenes, followed by a musical guest, more scenes, a fake news show, some scenes, another musical guest ... and a few more sketches—edgier ones as the hour grew nigh. (I later found out that these last sketches were called "ten-to-one" sketches because it was 12:50 a.m. and they could try more daring sketches at that time of night.)

Saturday Night Live can be broken down into sections that are ordered in a similar way each week.

> I love sketch comedy. My real goal is to do something with Albert Brooks. That would be my fantasy. I stay up night and day thinking up stuff he might find funny.
>
> Illeana Douglas

> If you want good sketches, go pick up Sid Caesar: The best of Your Show of Shows. That's the greatest sketch comedy you'll ever see on television.

Jamie Farr

The Second City, Chicago

I went back to college next semester and told friends about my epiphany. They told me to look into a place called The Second City, in Chicago, so I called and found out that they had a writing class taught by a former *Saturday Night Live* writer. Therefore, in 1990, I flew to Chicago with a bag of clothes and a computer and began studying sketch writing. The advice I got was, "Write it up and put it up," to see what it looks like. And when people would pitch ideas to each other, I would say, "WUSO" ("Write it up or shut up"). Ideas are a dime a dozen: you have to work on your ideas. If you don't, someone else will, because ideas have a very short shelf life. Everyone is looking for the same Easter eggs, and if you don't write or make your idea, eventually someone else will instead.

Chicago's The Second City has acted as incubator to all kinds of nascent improvisational comedy talent.

Writing for *Saturday Night Live*

Through the 1990s, I studied sketch writing, improv, and acting. I got hired by The Second City, and nine years after my epiphany, in August 1999, I was writing for *Saturday Night Live* during its 25th anniversary season. It took nine years to get there, and I did get in my own way numerous times (derailed by life), but eventually when I made that final push it took nine months. After my tenure on the show ended, they let go of three writers—the last three hired—because the network told them to cut their budget. And there it was, come and gone. The good news was that I was in New York—a challenging city to get to. I also had a craft and was part of a community of comedians.

Comedic analysis

In Chicago, people would ask me to look at their sketches when they were submitting for a job of some kind. I didn't realize it at the time, but I was teaching or script doctoring before I knew what that meant, so then I began teaching improv and writing classes. In the decade I have been in New York, and in the past two decades of doing this work, I have probably looked at more than 10,000 sketches. Therefore, I look at them the same way a radiologist would look at an X-ray: what's broken, what needs fixing, which bits seem pretty good, or with a few adjustments it's time to either put it up in front of a live audience, or videotape it, or put it aside for your packet. A packet is two to four sample sketches you have written to illustrate your writing. Plain and simple, it is a writing sample of what you would do if hired on a show.

The Peoples Improv, New York

I now live in New York. I have my own theater that was started in 2002. I teach there, perform there, in our new space—10,000 square feet of a comedy campus, with two theaters, a rehearsal space, green-screen room, voiceover booth, coffee shop, bar, and offices, all dedicated to the craft of comedy, improv, sketch, and solo performance. The theater is called the PIT, The Peoples Improv Theater, and we talk about the three Cs there: Craft, Community, Career. Work on your Craft and your Career will come, work on your Community and your Career will come. However, just work on your career and you will have neither a craft nor a community.

A PACKET

In order to get a job writing sketches, you need to have a packet, which consists of two to four sketches. (You should have at least a dozen in your arsenal, however.) Before you start worrying about agents and managers and stuff, at least two trusted friends should be able to say, "These are all very funny and you should be writing for that show."

THE EVOLUTION OF SKETCH COMEDY

If the oldest form of comedy is the caveman telling a funny story around the campfire, sketch comedy comes a close second. After a story gets recounted numerous times, however, it slowly loses its luster. No doubt it was recounted with vim and vigor and the caveman really sold it, much like a standup comedian, but listeners become restless hearing the same story repeatedly. So, at that point, one of the natural tools of storytelling must have been employed—exaggeration, the better part of storytelling. At that moment, the seeds of sketch comedy were sown, and our caveman discovered one of the earliest universal rules in comedy: if this, then what? Meaning, if this happened, then what else could have happened? A sketch comedian must extrapolate in order to further the events that actually took place.

A caveman gets to grips with some of the basic principles of comedy.

BE CREATIVE

The sample sketch below describes the finer points of sketch comedy. It is not meant to be performed; it is something that came to me as I ruminated on the first ever sketch. As a burgeoning sketch comedian, try to write things that you could create, either onstage or in a video—things that are doable. Let your premise (see page 172) and the dialogue do the work for you.

THE CAVEMAN SKETCH

Let's say there is a big strong caveman talking about what a man he is and how he is the strongest and bravest of all the cavemen. As he's talking, a woolly mammoth comes up behind him, his friends slowly back away, and when the caveman sees the animal he yells in fear and runs. Now let's assume that this is what happened. To make it into a sketch, we have to add a few more beats to it. We can keep the same truthful start: caveman makes pompous, overly confident speech of strength and power and then ... this is what needs to be made up for the sketch. In the real-life situation, the caveman ran away and that was the end of it.

What if, as the chase continued, instead of yelling he shrieked like some high-pitched animal, and then what if that shrieking turned into sobbing as he ran and then became all-out crying? He falls on the ground, gently rocking back and forth, moaning like a baby and sucking his thumb, at which point the woolly mammoth comes upon him and at first sight takes pity on him and his sad state, but then laughs and turns to walk away with a skip in its step, maybe whistling and smiling.

Now, we don't know if any of this happened. The caveman who was telling the story had to amp it up, because people had heard the retelling of the events, so what actually happened became embellished, and the first sketch began to be written ... theoretically.

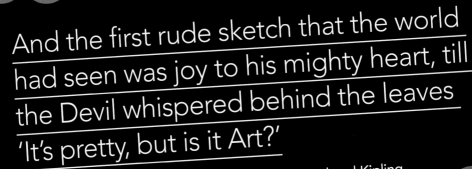

And the first rude sketch that the world had seen was joy to his mighty heart, till the Devil whispered behind the leaves 'It's pretty, but is it Art?'

Rudyard Kipling

So why does it work?

This is not a sketch I have ever written, done, seen, or improvised. As I said, I have included it here just to study the concepts of sketch. Having been a sketch comedian for more than two decades, I merely began with a story, an idea, a theory, a thought, a premise. "What was the first sketch ever created?" Then, using exaggeration, specificity, storytelling, heightening, and tightening, I have tried to "bend it, not break it." It includes three beats, which work well in sketch comedy—theater, art, and life. I had the story reach a crescendo and then fade out as the woolly mammoth walks away into the sunset.

"I DID SKETCH COMEDY FOR YEARS. I'VE ALWAYS ENJOYED IT."

JAMIE FARR

PLAYING FOR LAUGHS

Laughter is the sound of surprise, to explain why people are laughing at what they are laughing at. The audience's level of laughter is in direct proportion to how surprised they are by what you just said or did in the moment, assuming that it was well executed. Without derailing too much, performing comedy is not about what you say, but how you say it. So, for our purposes, let's assume that the execution is spot on. Mind you, the words need to be there, but in the wrong hands the words are useless and meaningless.

Sketch writers must go through many ideas before they find the ones they want to work on, because they are looking for surprising and unique ideas, concepts that have not been thought of, but yet when you see them, you wonder why no one else delved into this world to reveal what was so obvious.

A sketch from *Human Giant*, a comedy show that aired on MTV and featured many guest appearances.

At the end of the day, the role of any comedian is to entertain. Comedians have one goal in mind—they want to make you laugh. That is their mission, and they must accept that mission with aplomb and enthusiasm. Funny is a subjective thing, which is why there are so many different types of comedians, and why the comedian must find his or her audience. It begins with making friends and family laugh and then doing little shows for friends of friends and so on, until the audience grows through word of mouth. A good comedian is a satirist, though; one who can make you laugh but wants to make you think as well.

Sketch or story?

One might think that a caveman running from a woolly mammoth and shrieking is funny to other cavemen. Now if that's what happened, then that could be funny, but it's simply a funny story—it's not a sketch. It's storytelling, and that is the precursor to standup comedy. You are telling a funny story with your own twist on it. You are embellishing it a bit, recounting the details with joy, but essentially giving a rendition of the actual day's events.

First, there was storytelling around the fire; then the storyteller realized that honing the story and adding a few details for effect that may or may not have happened would help his story; then he realized that people were coming back to hear the story again around the fire so he decided to add beats to it to keep people entertained and happened upon the concept of the "rule of threes."

Bullyparade was a German sketch show from 1997–2002. Though no longer on air it has a cult following and has been compared to Monty Python's Flying Circus.

Three beats

In order for a sketch to be a sketch, it has to establish a premise, which is a theory or idea of what you think is funny and interesting and that you are going to set out to prove in your sketch (see page 172). It helps to have three beats, at least, that you may or may not make up, depending on the events. It needs to have an interesting turn of phrase, lingo, and specificity. So the caveman might have actually run away and maybe yelled a little, but you make him shriek, you make up that he cried, and that the woolly mammoth approached him as he was on his side crying like a baby. And woolly mammoths probably don't smile as they walk away, but in the sketch, you swear he did.

Good place to stop?

That would be a good place to end the sketch. Otherwise, we risk breaking it—as opposed to bending it. Once the bow is broken, it can no longer fire the arrow, but bent to its extremes it can bring down castles. So always aim your arrows high. In some people's opinions, we may have already broken it at numerous points, but that's one of the mandates of comedy—to push the envelope and boundaries of civilized society. Sketch comedy must risk being uncivilized. It is, after all, an absurd, abstract, exaggerated rendition of real or made-up events.

> You asked what is the secret of a really good sketch. A sketch is a small play. It's got a beginning, and a middle, and an end. It should have a plot; it should have the characters, conflict. It is a little play. And in it, will be funny stuff.
>
> Harvey Korman

THE PREMISE

All sketches begin with what we call a "comedy premise"—your theory of what you think is funny. You'll often hear people tell someone in the comedy business, "That would make for good material," or "You should do something with that," and they're right. Comedians should always be looking out for new material, just like artists always need to keep their eyes and ears open. Everything comes down to material, labor, and execution. A carpenter's material is wood … and with that wood and their labor, knowledge, and experience, they can make a beautiful piece of furniture. However, that piece of furniture will only be as nice as the wood they started with, and they have to work that material until the piece of furniture is ready to bring to market—the same is true for a comedian.

Prove your case

A premise, a theory—or, in legal terms, a case—must be proven. Sketch comedy writers can be likened to attorneys in this respect: they have a case to prove and, using evidence, they are going to prove it to you. The comedian's case is what they think is funny.

Gather all the evidence you can to make the case for your premise … it may need to stand up in court.

RHINO SKIN

A comedian's "workshop" is right in front of a load of people, and they have to feel comfortable when they fail in front of an audience. Therefore, to make it in show business, you really do need to have the skin of a rhino.

Keep a notebook (or similar) on your person at all times, for when inspiration strikes. Guard this "premise file" with your life.

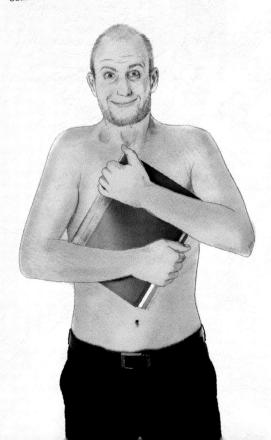

Take notes

If you want to be a comedian or comedy writer, carry something around with you to write with and write in. Then transfer your ideas to a premise file (something to keep your premises in), so when it's time to write you won't feel like you have to come up with an idea. Instead, you can look through your premise file, find a nice piece of comedy "wood," and begin to make something. When I was at *Saturday Night Live*, writers on the show would have 30- and 40-page premise files filled with ideas. Remember the wood analogy: your "furniture" will only be as good as the "wood" you begin with. It's important also to be able to synthesize your premise down to a sentence or two, so when you say it to someone, they get it immediately and hopefully think, "Now, that's funny."

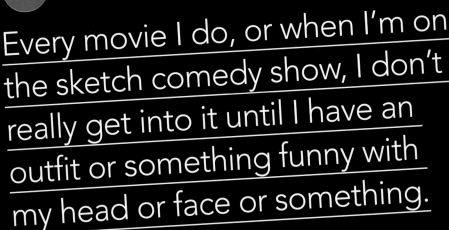

Every movie I do, or when I'm on the sketch comedy show, I don't really get into it until I have an outfit or something funny with my head or face or something.

Kel Mitchell

Different and well done

Seinfeld was my first guest on *Saturday Night Live*. I had an idea: "Seinfeld doing standup at the Last Supper." In one sentence you get it, and we can move on to "Let's see it executed." People (the general viewer, a producer) are looking for two things: Is there a cool, new, and different idea? And has it been executed well? You're better off having a cool idea that has not been well executed, however, because there is nothing worse than an unfunny, but well-delivered idea. You have to write down any, and every, idea that comes into your head, however spurious. For now you are just collecting ideas. Don't judge them—when you transcribe them into your premise file, you can decide which ones you want to hone into finely crafted vignettes.

Politics of the premise

Sketch comedy is essentially either social or political satire. Sketch comedians have chosen to speak truth by making people laugh, as opposed to preaching to them. Mind you, if it's not funny, that truth will fall flat. They are also shining the light of truth or consciousness on something that society has overlooked. Or they are turning the mirror back on society, showing people how they actually behave. They are really taking someone who has begun to take themselves too seriously down a peg or two. Perhaps that person has forgotten that he or she is like the rest of us.

To pursue a life in sketch comedy is to be an entertainer, to want to make people laugh (and maybe think). However, a sketch comedian is a satirist, who may employ parody—or hyperbole, or silliness—to enlighten us by being entertaining. Make us laugh and you might just make us think—maybe even change the world. Political figures are routinely spoofed and felled by sketch comedians. They take one aspect of the politician's personality and magnify it for comedic effect, often to the point where the audience thinks, "Yes, they are like that. I never really noticed that, but yes, that is really funny."

Les Trois Frères, 1995, had a simple premise: three brothers meet at their mother's funeral, spend their anticipated inheritance, then discover there is none ... the plot unfolds from there.

Structuring your case

Sketch comedians believe something is funny, and are going to prove it with exhibits a, b, and c and then get out. They will get to it sooner rather than later—hopefully by the bottom of page one, but if not, then definitely by page two. They are going to use specificity, because that's one of the simplest tools in the comedian's or artist's toolbox, and that's what takes a sketch from good to great. A candy bar is good, but a Willy Wonka super-duper chocolate bar is better.

SKETCH TYPES

The start of your sketch establishes some "who," "where," and maybe "what"—where is this sketch taking place, who are these people, and ultimately what is this sketch about? If sketch comedy can be divided into social or political satire, then it can also be divided into premise-driven and character-driven sketches.

EXAGGERATING CHARACTERS

A character-driven sketch can be one, or two, or more, characters speaking a certain way, and moving in a particular fashion. The accents, dialects, and mannerisms are all exaggerated, but hopefully create rich characters and not caricatures. As a performer, you are either playing "you plus" or a character. "You plus" is you, but you more articulate, awake, conscious. And so it goes with a sketch—the characters are straight (normal), and what they say is abnormal. This would be employing the tool of juxtaposition in comedy—seeing an old woman rapping or speaking in a street vernacular. The other side of the coin is when the characters are out-of-whack, slightly off-key, but what they are saying is normal and they take themselves very seriously.

John Cleese, in the Monty Python sketch "The Ministry of Silly Walks," perhaps one of the most well-known examples of exaggeration used to comic effect.

Character-based sketches

If this is the first time characters have been introduced, it's a character introduction sketch. We get their names and what they are about. We get a sense of their spine, their *modus operandi*, and maybe some turn of phrase or language that is unique to them. Once we've met these characters in the character introduction sketch, the "what" needs to be stronger. What is this sketch going to be about this time? We further both the language they first used and the physicality they exhibited initially.

Premise-driven sketches

An example of a premise-driven sketch is a doctor giving a female patient bad news regarding a delicate matter while using common street lingo to give the diagnosis. It is about being straight laced until the delicate info comes, and then it becomes street vulgar for a few words ("slapping" the audience),

Use exaggerated facial expressions to emphasize a character ... just don't get stuck like that.

and then switches back to medical language ("stroking" the audience), and then a further diagnosis with street lingo, thus slapping the audience. This is done three times, and we're out of there like a good little sketch comedian. It's about stroking the audience, then slapping, then stroke, stroke, stroke, slap, stroke, stroke, stroke, slap, stroke, stroke, stroke, slap, and get out of there.

WRITING YOUR SKETCH

The two hardest rules of comedy to master are: hold for laughs and leave them wanting more. As a performer you have to do both, but as a writer, you need only adhere to the second. A sketch needs to allow room for the reader, listener, and audience to have their own ideas of where it should, or could, go when they're done hearing it, as opposed to the audience thinking, "We get it. Now, get on with it and let's get to the next idea." If you choose to write down your sketches to be performed by others, your group, or as a sample packet to get a sketch writing job, there are certain ways to go about it.

Matt Lucas and David Walliams wrote and starred in *Little Britain*, a sketch show based on a selection of stereotypically British characters. However, the series also made a successful transition to the U.S. and Australia.

How to start …

What we see in any sketch is the brightest moment in the band of light that is the timeline between the players in our story. We don't need to know what the caveman was doing before coming upon the woolly mammoth who began chasing him, nor what the mammoth did after he walked off into the sunset. We must leave it alone, put down the pen.

… and how to finish

You could end it with the caveman on his side crying, or with the mammoth walking off in the sunset smiling and skipping. That is up to auteurs and, if they are lucky, they get to test it on live audiences numerous times to find out which is the best moment to end it. At a certain point, by the end of a sketch, you're never going to get a bigger response, and it's important to walk away at that moment—on top. When you get that last big laugh, run like the wind.

THE END

```
There are only two real ways to take
the lights out after a sketch. You
can either fade down the lights or
you can black them out (shut them
off completely, and immediately).
Usually, when you black out a
scene, it's because the ending is so
powerful that it's a button, and it
would be strange to fade down the
lights on such a moment.
```

> People will love something very much or hate something very much. But the great thing about a sketch show is that if something comes along that you don't like, something else will come along in a minute and hopefully you might like that.
>
> Matt Lucas

"

My friend Ali Farahnakian … wrote a very funny monologue about the McDonald's Big Mac—during the course of the monologue, he would eat an entire Big Mac extra value meal on stage. Because the meal was technically a prop, he made the stage manager buy it for him every night and he kept his $25 [per diem]. These were the kind of skills you learned touring for The Second City

Tina F

AHA! A.K.A. "LUNCHBOX"

Woman in a robe on stage. Man walks through in a hurry. Woman asks for a kiss. Man gives her one. Woman complains that was not enough. Man gives her more of a kiss. Man begins to walk out. Woman reminds him he has forgotten his lunch. He comes back to get it. She holds it behind her back using it as bait for an even more passionate kiss. He complies, and they mash and make a beast with two backs. Man grabs lunch and begins to run out the door. Woman says, "Have a nice day at school!" Man responds, "Thanks, Mom."

Reveal all

This sketch (left) was written in my youth at Chicago's The Second City. Such a short sketch needs a blackout (as opposed to a slow fade), so the audience is left in the dark, wondering what just happened. This is called a "reveal," because we think it is going to be one thing—husband and wife—and by the end, the last word or moment reveals that it has been something else entirely: mother and son. Another word for this sort of sketch is a "blackout."

Sketching it up!

Let's shift gears a little bit and discuss what to do with these ideas that have been coming to you. The first thing is to decipher the idea, to see if it is a sketch idea, a standup joke, a one-panel cartoon, or maybe a movie idea. How do you know? It takes time and critical thinking. Once you know it is a sketch idea, and that you want to work on it, there are various ways to attack it. You want to rip it from the ether and transform it into squiggly lines on paper that make sense to someone seeing (or reading) it.

CUTTING TO THE CHASE

Write a sketch the same way you would attend a cocktail party: get there late, and leave before you have worn out your welcome and people are over you. Often, when people write a sketch, the first few pages are just them getting warmed up, and invariably you can get rid of these pages and start where the first break in normalcy begins—the first fissure that lets us know something is different in this world. Unfortunately, most people want to linger too long in the "real world" of the sketch before they get to what the sketch is *about*.

Developing the concept

Here are some ways to deal with the idea you want to work on. Write your premise on an index card in as few words as possible—for example, "A diet pill that keeps you slightly nauseous for 12 to 16 hours so you won't eat." From there you make notes and brainstorm, free-form writing (or "morning pages"). Just start writing.

It may be a cliché but it's true—to be a writer you need to sit down and actually write ... even when you don't feel like it. Just do it.

Building blocks

You have to decide how you see this parody commercial being executed stylistically. Is it a polished pharmaceutical commercial, or a late-night advertisement? Once determined, begin to build on it. It could be three testimonials, or one person giving a testimonial and talking about three trigger foods, or it could be two ladies having lunch, where one says the other looks great, and the one who has lost weight says she has been taking a little pill. For now, let's call it "Ad Nauseam." We can come up with a better name later, but put something there—even "Insert joke here." As she describes her secret, she holds back the vomit. The social satire of this is the length we go just to lose weight, but that does not matter. Is it funny? Well executed? Did we leave them wanting more?

The write-up

You have made some notes and thought about your sketch. As Abraham Lincoln said, "Spend 80 percent of your time sharpening your ax and 20 percent cutting." It's now time to start writing it. Write a shoddy first draft—it's the best way to get started.

Liftoff

You have refined your idea to its essence, resulting in a powerful high-concept premise that is understandable to others when you say the few sentences. You've made notes, in which are your three examples—reasons why you think the premise is funny. The examples heighten and tighten and build to a crescendo, and then you're out, or you may have a dénouement or a button at the end. OK, it's time to start writing.

STORYBOARD IT!

Another technique is to describe the sketch in slides or storyboards. So you would have: "Woman in restaurant, friend joins her, they hug and sit, woman one is obviously impressed by woman two, as woman two begins to speak about the diet pill she is obviously nauseous," etc.

Sometimes thinking about a sketch visually can help—and drawing up a storyboard will certainly help you communicate your idea to others.

Drafting

The first draft is panning for gold. Take your thoughts and notes, and let them spew from your mind. Don't over-think things: let the characters do the talking—get out of the way and take dictation for them, see how they react to the imaginary circumstances you have placed them in. It should not seem like work. Feel the energy. Say, "This is fun!" Giggle at what you're writing. Some good things are coming, but don't pat yourself on the back—keep calm and carry on.

Sketcher–farmer, or sketch farming

Once you are done with the first draft, go through it and do the farming (a.k.a. editing). The first draft is hunter–gatherer. You have a plan and, once you start, it goes out the window and the writing/typing begins. If only one sentence or phrase makes it to the second draft, that's a victory. All of a sudden, you are typing the words "fade out" or "blackout." You've done it: you've written a sketch, most likely a shoddy one, but now you have something to work on.

Once you get going, don't stop, just get it all down. But feel free to have some fun along the way—go on, enjoy yourself!

Editing

Leave your draft alone for a bit. Come back to it with fresh eyes and try to read it as if you were editing a friend's sketch. Read it once and make notes. Where does the sketch begin? Does it make sense? Where are the jokes? Circle them. Where are the three beats? Do you get to "it" soon enough? All of this presumes that the premise is solid. Then you begin to edit, eliminating as much fat as possible, leaning it up for market. Filet of sketch is what people are looking for. Open on, and then into dialogue, until fade out, with very few (if any) departures for stage directions, or—heaven forbid—telling actors what they should be doing or feeling. Sketch writers are paid for their ideas and their execution, and the cool dialogue, lingo, and turn of phrase within the sketch. After the first draft, you may want to research the language other diet pill companies use and vomiting terminology.

> If I don't have a project going, I sit down and begin to write something—a character sketch, a monologue, a description of some sight, or even just a list of ideas.
>
> Thomas Perry

> # If you want to be an actor, you need to learn how to act first, even in sketch comedy.
>
> Nicole Sullivan

The oral tradition

You may not even have to write down sketch comedy if you have no desire to get a job in sketch writing, and just want to perform it with friends and make videos. You can have the premise or scenario, and then go out there and try that premise in front of a live audience (or the cameras) until you have something you want to put out there.

Oral sketch

One of my alma maters, The Second City, had more of an oral tradition of sketch comedy. An actor will have an idea, and he or she will ask another person to be in this idea or premise with him or her. They will go out that night and try that premise in front of a live audience and, if it gets some laughs and works on some level, they'll try it again the next night. And if it keeps working, they'll keep doing it until opening night, when it goes into the show ... yet the actors have never had a script to create this piece. They have taken a thought and turned it into a living thing.

Spontaneous again

As a performer, when you do "sketchprov"—the hybrid of sketch and improv, because you know your premise and your character, but don't know where it might go—you'll remember the next night what worked and what didn't. You will keep the good stuff, tinker with it, then leave it alone, and get rid of the mediocre. Craig Taylor, stage manager of The Second City's main stage for over 30 years, will say to the cast as they are about to try sketches they've done the night before, "Let's be spontaneous all over again." You don't even have to know how to read and write to do sketch comedy.

Improvisation is a great way to try out material and get an immediate feel for whether or not it's working. And you never know where collaborative ideas might lead.

"IT'S LESS LONELY. SKETCH COMEDY IS MUCH MORE FUN THAN STANDUP. YOU CAN STILL HAVE A GOOD TIME WHEN YOU'RE BOMBING IN SKETCH COMEDY BECAUSE AT LEAST YOU'RE BOMBING WITH OTHER PEOPLE."

DAVE FOLEY

BECOMING SUCCESSFUL

As I said earlier, and it merits repeating, work on your craft and your career will come. Work on your community and your career will come. But just try to work on your career, and you'll have neither a craft nor a community. If you're not ready for your shot, it will just make you look silly. Practice your craft, write, take improv classes to become a better writer, form sketch groups, put up your stuff, and make videos. Do it because you love it—because it's fun, because it's your way of expressing yourself—and if you're lucky, maybe your hobby can be your profession. And don't take yourself too seriously. After all, we're here to entertain and maybe "edutain" (educate and entertain) each other while doing time on planet Earth.

Practice your craft wherever you can find a captive audience.

> "BECAUSE THERE ARE FEWER PARAMETERS [IN IMPROV] THAN ANY OTHER PERFORMING ART, YOU MUST BE PREPARED FOR ANYTHING THAT COMES YOUR WAY. THAT INCLUDES FORAYS INTO THE WORLDS OF WRITING, DIRECTING, DESIGN, DANCE, MUSIC, SINGING, MIME, STAGE COMBAT, AND ESPECIALLY ACTING. ONCE YOU'VE GOT ALL OF THESE DOWN, THEN YOU CAN SAY THAT IMPROV IS EASY."
>
> JEFF CATANESE

Get it out there

If you want to be a writer, write down your ideas. Then, once a week, transform one into a sketch. Don't romanticize this work; it's a wonderful job, where hopefully you get to do good, and do well. Become a student of the craft, watching and reading as much sketch as possible. Become a content-producing machine. Don't care about quality in the beginning. Don't let perfect become the enemy of good: make stuff, art by the pound, and sooner or later something will happen. What that will be, time will tell. As they say, tragedy plus time equals comedy. All we can control is the time and the comedy, how long we wait, and the comedy we can draw from it. Hopefully, we are able to harness the universality in the room and the world regarding a topic. We can speak truth to the moment and garner energy in the form of a laugh.

Share the truth

People do not laugh at people trying to be funny—they laugh at people being truthful, and funny is a byproduct of truth. Go out there and share your truth. It may make people laugh or cry, but both are good. It might even make them laugh so hard they shriek. Oh yeah: another great comedy tool is the callback. A callback is recalling something that was said or done earlier in a sketch that the audience may have forgotten about, and when you call it back, they are reminded of it and potentially it may garner a laugh. It's a great way to end something—which, by the way, is the hardest thing to do in art. The end.

ALI REZA FARAHNAKIAN

Owner of the Peoples Improv Theater (*www.ThePIT-NYC.com*) in New York City, founded in 2002, where he also teaches and performs, Ali is also an alumnus of the ImprovOlympic, The Second City, and *SNL*. He has been in numerous films, television shows, and commercials, as well as some plays. Google him. If you're ever in New York, come by the PIT to say hello.

8
WRITING SITCOMS

It is possible to make a living as a sitcom writer. It's also possible to become the next James L. Brooks or Johnny Speight. But talent is only a small part of the success equation. Along with talent, you must have knowledge. And there's a lot to learn: script format, character development, television production lingo, submission procedures, and on and on … And then there's perhaps the most important bit: networking. Fortunately, the technical information is available. You don't have to join a secret society to learn all you need to know. As for networking, there's an old saying: "It's not what you know, but who you know." In the case of sitcom writing, it's what you know and who you know. You could be the best sitcom scriptwriter the world has ever known. But if you don't put yourself in close proximity to the people who matter, your talent won't matter.

READ SCRIPTS

If you're thinking of creating a sitcom script, probably the best way to begin is to get a sitcom script and read it! Then read it again. There are hundreds online: you may have to hunt for them, but they are out there. They will often be posted in pdf format, which makes them easy to print out. Having a script in your hands just makes the idea of writing one seem that much more possible.

CAUTION

Printing out scripts may violate copyright laws ... or it may fall under "fair use." No one seems to be able to agree, but we're not aware of anyone being prosecuted for printing out a sitcom script for study purposes.

Form a scriptwriting group to share info and get feedback on your script-in-progress.

Script stores

Stores in Hollywood offer scripts for sale. They have shelves bursting with scripts—old, recent, pilots, unproduced, original—all reasonably priced. You can also find them available for purchase on eBay, many of them offered by script collectors, and often on "Buy it Now," rather than on auction.

These abbreviations represent the writers' guilds in the U.K., U.S., Australia, and Canada. All have web sites, and offer tremendous resources for nonmembers as well as members.

o www.writersguild.org.uk For a reasonable fee, even writers who haven't had anything produced or published can join the Writers' Guild of Great Britain. Members are entitled to Guild publications, phone advice, and access to a free contract-vetting service. The WGGB site and blog also offer inside information and podcasts on a variety of topics.

o wga.org The Writers Guild of America site offers an eye-popping list of resources for nonmembers. Just clicking on the "writing for episodic TV" link under the "Writer's Resources" button leads to a list of PDFs that walk an aspiring writer through the process of writing scripts for television. Dozens of articles explain technical jargon, script mechanics, and technological advances. Multiple links lead to lists of agents, contest opportunities, training programs, and even more links!

o www.awg.com.au The membership cost of the Australian Writers' Guild is based on writers' income—if you make less, you pay less. Joining is the best way to gain access to industry information and a range of services. Members can even purchase a discounted version of Final Draft, the scriptwriting software that is the industry standard.

o www.wgc.ca The Writers Guild of Canada offers nonmembers a menu of resources related to scriptwriting, including partial reprints of feature articles from the Guild's Canadian Screenwriter Magazine, as well as links to lawyers, agents, and other online industry resources, such as blogs, industry organizations, and government film and television agencies.

SCRIPTWRITING BOOKS

There are hundreds of books that review, in minute detail, every aspect of television scriptwriting. Many are written by actual, working television writers and producers, so they provide some insight into the inner workings of the television business, as well as comprehensive information on actually writing a script.

Eventually you have to put the book down and actually start writing your script.

WRITING BIBLE

Ellen Sandler's *TV Writer's Workbook: A Creative Approach to Television Scripts* advises aspiring sitcom writers on the mechanics of sitcom scriptwriting, how to "break down" a script—even how to approach agents and managers. Sandler was nominated for an Emmy as co-executive producer of the hit series *Everybody Loves Raymond*, so she knows what she's talking about.

Read, read, read

It's also a good idea to read show-business books—biographies, autobiographies, tell-all books, nonfiction books by writers, producers, directors, and actors involved in television production. Eventually, if you read enough of them, you'll get an idea of how the entertainment business works. *Script* magazine—both the printed and online version—is published six times a year, and offers timely articles on the film and television industry.

Ugly Betty translated beautifully from one country to another to another to another.

WRITING SCRIPTS FOR TV SHOWS

Don McEnery is a standup comic, writer, and actor, whose *Seinfeld* script was nominated for an Emmy. His film-writing credits include co-writing *A Bug's Life*, *Hercules*, and *Stuart Little: Call of the Wild*. As a comic, he's appeared on *Star Search*, *An Evening at the Improv*, and *Stand-Up Spotlight*, and he performs in Los Angeles, Las Vegas, New York, and Atlantic City. *The Tape* (season three, episode eight) was nominated for Outstanding Individual Achievement in Writing in a Comedy Series.

READ, LISTEN, WATCH

There has been an explosion of free, reliable, and detailed information on the Internet about writing sitcom scripts. Writers, producers, and show runners chronicle their experiences, their frustrations, and their triumphs in blog form, providing unprecedented peeks into the inner workings of television. Podcasts dedicated to the business and lifestyle of scriptwriting feature interviews with experienced writers and producers. There are also videotaped interviews and lectures on sites such as YouTube and Vimeo that deal with scriptwriting and producing. The Internet is full of people who have valuable information and are willing to share it.

The Internet is bursting with helpful information about scripts—writing them, pitching them, polishing them, and selling them.

Be on your guard

There are also unscrupulous people, as well. Some will offer to critique or assess a script, often claiming to evaluate whether it has a chance of getting produced. Sometimes, they'll offer the service for a fee. Many of these are legitimate services, but some are not. On rare occasions, they'll steal your script or take your money and not give back anything in return.

EXPORTING PHIL

The 2010 documentary *Exporting Raymond* follows *Everybody Loves Raymond* creator Phil Rosenthal to Moscow as he attempts to turn his long-running American hit sitcom into a Russian sitcom. The movie depicts how cultural differences can affect the way that comedy is presented.

Often, classrooms are good places to learn the basics of scriptwriting. Extension campuses, adult education programs, or major universities offer courses or workshops that provide instruction and guidance in scriptwriting. Some even serve as a conduit for various fellowships or intern programs that afford select students further opportunity to gain a close-up look at television or film production. Instruction, feedback, script evaluation, and other resources usually form part of any good scriptwriting class.

Every aspiring scriptwriter hopes to hit the jackpot with a long-running sitcom.

MARRIED WITH CHILDREN, RUSSIAN STYLE

Married with Children was popular on U.S. television for 11 years, and now it's very popular in Russia. But is it the same show? Sort of—it's an "authorized copy" of the original. In Russia, *Married with Children* is now *Schastlivy Vmeste*, which translates to "Happy Together." Al and Peg Bundy are now Gena and Dasha Bukin, and Chicago is now Yekaterinburg. But the satire, vulgarity, and plot themes remain the same.

In the old days, scriptwriters required a lot of paper, Wite-Out, and patience. Software eliminates the need for two of the three.

SCRIPTWRITING SOFTWARE

Scripts follow a very specific format, and they must be submitted in that format—no questions asked. In the past, using a conventional typewriter, it was a tedious and time-consuming task to write a script while adhering to the eccentricities of television script layout. No longer … Using a computer, and any of a number of software programs, it has never been easier to concentrate on the dialogue while letting the computer take care of the formatting.

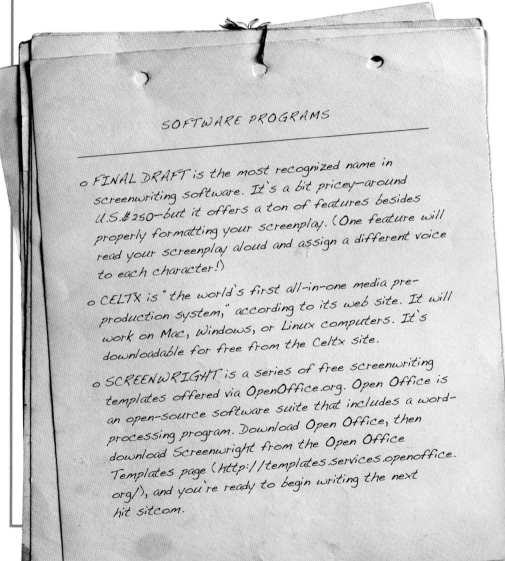

SOFTWARE PROGRAMS

o FINAL DRAFT is the most recognized name in screenwriting software. It's a bit pricey—around U.S.$250—but it offers a ton of features besides properly formatting your screenplay. (One feature will read your screenplay aloud and assign a different voice to each character!)

o CELTX is "the world's first all-in-one media pre-production system," according to its web site. It will work on Mac, Windows, or Linux computers. It's downloadable for free from the Celtx site.

o SCREENWRIGHT is a series of free screenwriting templates offered via OpenOffice.org. Open Office is an open-source software suite that includes a word-processing program. Download Open Office, then download Screenwright from the Open Office Templates page (http://templates.services.openoffice.org/), and you're ready to begin writing the next hit sitcom.

THE LAUGH TRACK

Invented in 1953, the laugh track at one time supplied the laughter for 80 percent of the comedies on television. It is used sparingly, if at all, these days, having fallen into disrepute over the past two decades. Writing in 1990, Paul Krassner said that so-called "canned laughter" is "the lowest form of fascism. It is propaganda that falsely—almost subliminally—implies something is funny when it isn't. It is TV's ultimate insult to the audience." Standup comics (one of which Krassner claims to be) are well aware of the vagaries of crowd dynamics. When only one audience member laughs, it can be rather uncomfortable ... for him, for the comic, or for the rest of the audience, which is silent. But when that cascade of laughter comes—when the entire room laughs after being kick-started by the first audience member to get to the heart of the punch line—it's great. That first laugher is the one who essentially gives the audience "permission" to guffaw. Now multiply that situation by millions, an audience watching at home, and you begin to see the genius of canned laughter. If it had been devised in the age of the Internet, it would have been called a "virtual audience" rather than "canned laughter."

> Nobody is as innocent as they used to be. You can't work in a world of wish fulfillment. This is an adult family comedy. You have to have some honesty and edge to be successful. We're reflecting existing behavior, not encouraging it.
>
> Bruce Helford, producer of
> *The Drew Carey Show*

WRITE A SPEC SCRIPT ...
THEN ANOTHER

A "spec" script is a script that's written "on spec"—short for "on speculation."
In other words, it hasn't been solicited or commissioned. It is a script you write to
demonstrate your skills as a writer, showing that you know how to write a script and
are familiar with the conventions of scriptwriting. Another name would be a sample
script. They rarely get purchased or prowduced—that isn't what they are for.

Spec scripts

A spec script is usually written for
a television show that is currently
airing, often for a show that is
popular among viewers and critics.
If you were to write a script for
a show that no one watches or
no one cares about, then the
person evaluating your script
won't be familiar enough with
the program to make a fair
assessment of your skills.

"COMEDY ALWAYS
WORKS BEST WHEN IT
IS MEAN-SPIRITED."

JOHN CLEESE

Left to right: Jennifer Saunders,
Julia Sawalha, and Joanna Lumley,
the cast of *Absolutely Fabulous*.

- The hit 1970s sitcom All in the Family was based on Till Death Us Do Part. The U.S. version was the crowning achievement of producer Norman Lear and actor Carroll O'Connor. Johnny Speight created the U.K. version and its star, Warren Mitchell (as Alf Garnett), went on to a distinguished career in stage and television.

- Three's Company was Man about the House in England.

- Dear John was Dear John, making the transition from England to America without the traditional name change.

- Two different attempts at remaking Fawlty Towers failed in the U.S. Amanda's, starring Bea Arthur—a re-do which changed the name of the series as well as the gender of the main character—flopped. Payne, starring John Larroquette, did not catch on with American viewers. Perhaps America would have preferred to see a Fawlty Towers starring John Cleese.

- The U.S. version of Australia's Kath and Kim failed miserably, and a version of Absolutely Fabulous is always rumored to be in the making. However, American viewers will always be partial to Jennifer Saunders and Joanna Lumley, having been exposed to the pair and their drunken antics on at least four different U.S. television outlets.

THE OFFICE

When *The Office* first aired in Britain in 2001, it's doubtful whether star and creator Ricky Gervais knew he would be creating something that would become a worldwide cultural phenomenon. Now, versions of *The Office* are airing all around the globe. In France, it's called *Le Bureau*. In Germany, it's *Stromberg*. The Brazilians watch *Os Aspones*. In America, it's called *The Office* and stars Steve Carell in the David Brent/Ricky Gervais role. *The Office* isn't the only British sitcom to translate well to American audiences.

First-time flukey?

Writing more than one spec script is a good idea—after all, the first script you wrote might have just been a fluke. You may have gotten extraordinarily lucky. In order to counteract that, you will need to write a second spec script, and this will leave no one in any doubt about your ability.

Dreams on Spec was a 2007 American documentary film that profiles the struggles and triumphs of emerging Hollywood screenwriters.

"As an insider's guide for screenwriters trying to crash the gates, DREAMS ON SPEC is - pardon the expression - pitch perfect."
Steven de Souza, Screenwriter, 48 HOURS, DIE HARD, & LARA CROFT

Dreams on Spec

Every year screenwriters finish tens of thousands of scripts, but only a few hundred are made into movies.

Choose a live one

It is advisable to write a script for a show that you are intimately familiar with. It is also prudent to write a script for a show that is not in imminent danger of cancellation. If that happens, it's back to the computer to write another spec script. It's bad form to send along a spec script for a show that's no longer on the air.

SERIES VS. SEASON

When Americans talk about television, "series" refers to the show itself. The word "season" is the specified time that the series runs on the prime-time schedule. The season runs roughly from September to May. In the past, networks have most often committed to 13—sometimes 26—episodes. In the U.K., "series" is used the same way that Americans use "season." Broadcasters usually commit to far fewer episodes than in American television, sometimes commissioning production of only six episodes. So, to review: an American television viewer might settle in to watch the fifth season of his favorite series, while a British television fan would be watching series five of his favorite program.

Do your research

Once you've chosen a show, watch every episode you can. Watch one or two or three episodes repeatedly. Become familiar with the characters, their speech patterns, their motivations, their relationships. It is also helpful to know the settings back-to-front. Don't put your characters in a rocket ship to the moon if most of the scenes take place in a living room, a coffee shop, and a warren of office cubicles. Don't write a script that calls for a guest appearance by Sir John Gielgud or the USC Marching Band, or that calls for elaborate special effects or expensive sets. Don't throw adult humor into a family show. Most of this is common sense, but it needs to be stated. Or, you can write an original script.

By reading a script aloud, before a live audience at a film festival (such as the 17th Annual Austin Film Festival, above), a screenwriter can garner valuable feedback.

WRITE AN ORIGINAL SCRIPT

An original sample script not only demonstrates an ability to write a sitcom script. It also showcases your ability to develop an original concept for a show, and create and develop characters—all while working within the conventions of sitcom production.

Pilot scripts

The BBC specifically states that it won't accept scripts based on existing shows. It wants to see scripts that are original and that also include the authors' ideas on how they see the show developing. In other words, the BBC wants to see a "pilot script"—a script that sets up the show, establishes the setting, introduces characters, and sets the entire series in motion.

WRITERSROOM

The BBC regularly solicits original scripts through its BBC writersroom web site. Writersroom "is always on the lookout for fresh, new, talented writers for a changing Britain. When we find them, we do everything we can to get their voice heard and their work produced."

Familiarize yourself with terms like "pilot script," "story arc," and "show bible."

Hearing an actor read your words can give you a good idea of what works—and what doesn't.

Submitting a script

Once you have written your script, don't send it to any entity, network, or agency unsolicited (unless, as in the case of the BBC writersroom, it specifically solicits materials). Most will merely send it back unopened. They do this for very good reason—to protect themselves against charges of misappropriation. If producers were to open unsolicited scripts, they would set themselves up to charges down the line. In the rare case a producer or executive will agree to look at a piece of work, it would necessarily be after a "submission agreement" is signed that absolves the agent or exec from any liability. But how to get the script into the hands of someone who can do something with it?

LAST OF THE SUMMER WINE

The longest-running sitcom in history first premiered in 1973 in England on BBC1. The final episode aired in 2010. Astonishingly, every single episode was written by one man— Roy Clarke.

NETWORKING, CONTESTS, MANAGEMENT

How do you get the script from your printer to the network executive? Networking is good—knowing people who know people who know other people. It's not an exact science, but it's true and it's real. Perform regularly at comedy clubs or in improv troupes in a major city, as these venues serve as entertainment nexuses.

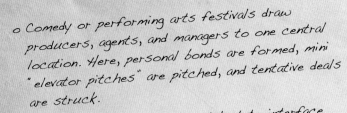

- Comedy or performing arts festivals draw producers, agents, and managers to one central location. Here, personal bonds are formed, mini "elevator pitches" are pitched, and tentative deals are struck.

- Contests efficiently allow talent to interface with industry. Scriptwriting contests attract talented people desiring a scriptwriting career to get their output into the hands of the people that matter.

- Internships get you near the folks that can make things happen—all while you gain intimate knowledge of the inner workings of the entertainment industry. They are often unpaid and involve long hours.

- Spend some money and shoot a short segment based on your script. This will get it noticed and possibly secure management or representation. Then upload it to YouTube or FunnyOrDie.

Standup TV

Standup comics have been the natural choice as stars of American television networks since TV's "golden age." Many of the early hit shows were merely productions based on fully formed concepts that had been produced for years on radio. And many of them starred comedians—Lucille Ball, Jack Benny, and George Burns, to name just a few. Comedians who had been honing and polishing acts and personas in comedy clubs, nightclubs, and other venues since the 1930s were logical choices to star in early comedies or sketch shows. Often they had the necessary acting skills and timing to carry sitcoms.

Famous shows often do a script reading at film or comedy festivals. The "table read" is an integral part of sitcom production.

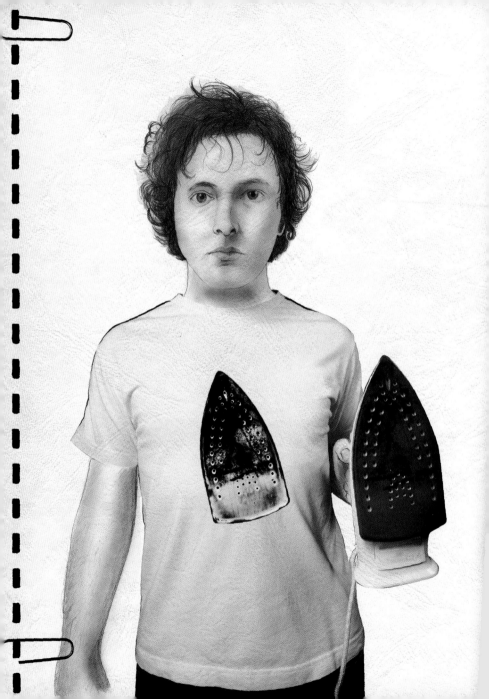

9
PRINT HUMOR

Crafting and performing humorous monologues is just one way to express yourself creatively and with humor. There are dozens of avenues for expression in existence, and more are being launched at a frantic pace. In the last decade or so, the ways to create and distribute this mirth have gone through a technological revolution (and we don't use that word loosely). The revolution is far from over. The magazines, books, and other publications that adorn newsstands and library racks have an appetite for humorous content, and they regularly solicit and accept manuscripts, short-form essays, jokes, gags, or captions from freelancers. In-flight magazines, house organs, radio comedy services, technical magazines, book publishers, manufacturers of novelty items (T-shirts, hats, mugs, etc.)—all of them use humorous material … and all of it must be created by someone. Often it's purchased from "outside sources."

DIY

Changes are afoot. The Internet is causing nearly all producers of the written word to change their respective models. This same Internet is enabling every single individual citizen to be his or her own publishing house, novelty item producer, movie studio, or radio producer. The means of production and distribution are within reach of an ever-expanding number of people, and the costs of production continue to plummet.

New media allows creators to interface directly with consumers, thereby skipping the middle man ... or woman.

Spread sidewise

Not everyone has a burning desire to be a performer. And not everyone wants to move to one of the entertainment capitals of the world in order to pursue a Golden Globe. Many people would prefer to simply make a living (or supplement their income) by creating humor in one or more of its various forms. Those who do perform might want to bulk up their résumés or enhance their reputations by displaying versatility in one or more of the visual arts or in print media. There's no rule that says that a comedy performer can't diversify. Some of the following creative endeavors might not be lucrative. Some may result in absolutely no remuneration at all. However, they may provide a showcase for your sense of humor, which could lead to other opportunities.

Twitter gives the power to foment a political uprising ... or launch a comedy career.

TWITTER

Twitter was created in 2006. It is a social networking site that enables its 200 million users to engage in "microblogging." Users open a Twitter account, which allows them to post 140-character (maximum!) "tweets," which are visible to other Twitter users, either through the Twitter web site (on the user's profile) or via cell phone. Around 65 million tweets are sent every day, and by accessing such tweets, users can share what is happening in their lives at a particular moment or they can publish opinions, poems, jokes, or links to online stories. Users can subscribe to other people's tweets by becoming a "follower" or "tweep" (a blend of "Twitter" and "peep"). If it can be expressed in fewer than 140 characters, it can be tweeted.

"hoever said that things have to be useful?

Evan Williams, Twitter co-founder and CEO

Show off!

Even though you may not end up as a media superstar, Twitter can give you the chance to perfect the crafting of concise nuggets of comedy. With hard work, together with networking and promotion, your Twitter account can become a showcase for your humor-writing talent.

USER-GENERATED CONTENT

It's one of the most important phrases of the first decade of the 21st century. "User-gen" for short, it describes any photos, news, videos, blogs, podcasts—anything—that is uploaded and shared via the Internet. The term makes the distinction between content generated by regular people ("users") and content produced by traditional generators, such as movie studios or television networks or publishing houses or newspapers. If someone can read it, watch it, view it, or listen to it, then it's "content." Put another way, if it can help you waste time at work, it's content. For most small-time content generators, the initial idea isn't mass-market fame or any ensuing fortune. It's purely for artistic expression or the imparting of knowledge. If the content finds a "market" (that is, if more than just your friends or relatives watch/view/read it), so much the better. If it attracts the attention of traditional media—and they can figure out how to turn your niche content into a product, that can then be distributed via traditional channels—then congratulations! You have hit the cyber jackpot.

WHAT NEXT FOR JUSTIN?

Justin Halpern, a 29-year-old comedy writer, moved to Hollywood, tried his hand at screenwriting, but met with limited success. He was employed as a writer for *Maxim Online* web site when he moved back to his native San Diego to live with his parents. According to most accounts, Halpern had always kept a record of his cantankerous septuagenarian father's salty comments. But in 2009, he decided to publish them using Twitter. His Twitter bio reads: "I'm 29, I live with my 74-year-old dad. He is awesome. I just write down shit that he says." From that humble beginning, in August 2009, Halpern embarked on a legendary show-business journey. The Twitter account garnered mentions online and in the traditional media, which led to 700,000 subscribers. Simon & Schuster saw the potential of such a large audience and published a book, *Sh*t My Dad Says*, in May 2010. This in turn caught the attention of CBS television, which eventually produced a hit sitcom based on the Twitter feed and the book. That television program launched just 13 months later and is attracting respectable audiences in its time slot. His Twitter account has more than two million followers.

Twitter co-founders (from left) Evan Williams, Biz Stone, and Jack Dorsey photographed in their offices in downtown San Francisco.

CYBER-CENSOR YOURSELF?

Not everyone will be amused by your tweets:

"I was born without a censor button. My mouth and now e-mail will continue to get me into trouble."

Gilbert Gottfried, just after getting fired as the voice of the AFLAC Duck. His controversial tweets joked about the Sendai tsunami and were deemed unacceptable by his employer.

T-SHIRTS/CAFÉ PRESS

T-shirts emblazoned with humorous sayings and/or illustrations don't write themselves. If you have an idea for a T-shirt you think might be a best seller, here are your options.

1. Purchase silk-screening equipment, burn the screen, and print the T-shirts. Then sell via a web site (or in publications read by people who might like your T-shirt) or directly to the public—at fairs, outside of stadiums, anywhere a crowd gathers. The equipment, advertising, and sales license will cost money, lots of it. You'll have to take care of fulfillment (taking orders, taking money, and sending the product to the purchaser)

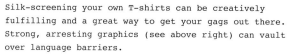
Silk-screening your own T-shirts can be creatively fulfilling and a great way to get your gags out there. Strong, arresting graphics (see above right) can vault over language barriers.

and you'll also have to store the shirts while you're waiting for them to fly off the shelves—unless you can find a retailer to sell them for you. (The retailer takes a cut, and you get what's left over after subtracting expenses.) Don't forget to buy the blank T-shirts.

2. Contract with a silk-screen company and have it print your shirts (see above for sales strategies). Again, this method is costly, but less time is spent physically printing shirts.

3. Log on to Café Press or similar, create your shirt, then have it create a virtual store. Your cut will be smaller than with other methods, but you won't be doing any of the production or fulfillment.

4. Sell your idea to a company buying ideas for T-shirts. You'll only get $50 or $100, and you'll sign away all rights to the idea/slogan/graphic. However, you'll be free to dream up other ideas and won't get inky hands.

Promo T

If you want the T-shirt to sell, you have to do some promotion—press releases (hopefully, humorous ones!), advertising (online or offline), promoting through social networking (blogging or tweeting), or wearing it while walking downtown.

SAME GIG FOR GEWGAWS ...

These ideas also apply to hats, buttons, mouse pads, knickknacks, gewgaws, doodads, tchotchke, or any other novelty item you might dream up. Numerous silk-screening outfits can put your graphic or gag on anything—and we mean anything. They don't buy ideas: they're all about providing customers with promotional products, usually in vast quantities. There are smaller outfits that sell preprinted merchandise, nearly all of which have web sites. Some actually purchase jokes or slogans.

GREETINGS CARDS

Major greeting card companies have full-time in-house staff writing copy. Write to them and ask if they are accepting freelance work; they might look to buy material from time to time. Smaller companies often accept freelance submissions, but it's always advisable to contact them first to discover their freelance policy and requirements for submissions. Keep in mind that they'll most likely want batches of ideas—perhaps as many as one or two dozen at a time. While they appreciate genius, prodigious output is prized.

NONFICTION BOOKS

If you want to sell an idea for a humorous, nonfiction book, at the very least you need to have a book proposal. And if you want to get a fiction book published, you have to provide a prospective publisher with a completed manuscript. There are countless books, blogs, web sites, and magazine articles out there that spell out exactly how to create a book proposal. Writers love to write about writing. The secret to a successful book proposal is no secret. It's out there.

British comedian Sheridan Simove wrote a best seller, *What Every Man Thinks About Apart From Sex*, which contained nothin' but 200 blank pages!

Book proposals

These follow rather specific guidelines. If you are at all serious about appearing serious, then it's worthwhile doing some research on how they're created. We couldn't possibly cover everything that needs to go into a book proposal in the limited space that we have here. However, a proposal will contain, at the very least, an overview of the book, a biography of the author, the structure of the book, plus a sample chapter (or even two or three chapters). Plus a whole lot more. It is really important to do it correctly. An inadequate book proposal will be summarily rejected—even if the idea behind the proposal is a great one.

Sir Pelham Grenville Wodehouse had a career that spanned 70 years, and much of his work is read and admired to this day.

Ninety-nine percent of fiction in America is serious. England has more of a tradition of comic writing—P. G. Wodehouse (who actually wrote in America), Noël Coward, Evelyn Waugh, Kingsley Amis, and more recently Ben Elton, Stephen Fry, Helen Fielding, and Nick Hornby.

Rita Rudner

SELF-PUBLISHING

Self-publishing—commissioning a publishing house (a "vanity press") to proofread, typeset, print, and bind your book—has been around for a very long time. Some famous authors are alleged to have borne the cost of publishing one or two of their books. Apparently, if not common practice, it was an accepted practice. In modern times, however, self-publishing can carry a stigma. The reasoning went that, if you self-published your book, that must mean that no one wanted to publish it … and therefore that it wasn't worth buying or reading.

Ben Franklin was one of the "founding fathers" of self-publishing. His *Poor Richard's Almanack* was one of the colonies' first "best sellers," with 10,000 in annual sales.

Big time second time

When a handful of these vanity productions actually sold well, that all changed. At least, they sold well enough to gain the attention of mainstream publishers, who subsequently bought the rights to the books. Then they reissued them, and promoted and distributed them with even greater success.

E-books

Another technological advance is the e-book, which can be read on the popular Kindle portable e-book reader or other similar device, like an iPhone, or a PC or other desktop computer. There is now a method by which an author can submit a manuscript to *amazon.com* and publish the work merely by "marking up" the text using simple HTML mark-up language. The author sets the price of the e-book and Amazon keeps a portion of the proceeds, and the rest goes to the author. Since there are significantly smaller productions costs—compared to offset printing or print on demand—there is more profit for the retailer, the author, and/or publisher.

Disintermediation

As with most new technologies, such methods "disintermediate" the traditional publishers—that is, they "cut out the middle man." The author (theoretically, at least) doesn't have to submit a manuscript to a publisher, or figure out how to get the book pumped through

ON DEMAND

One factor that changed self-publishing was technology (of course!)—specifically, publishing on demand. Also called print on demand, this process enables an author to publish a book in smaller quantities and with lower set-up costs.

the various retail channels. Nor is the publisher required to mount gaudy, expensive advertising and promotional campaigns in print or on television and radio … because the publisher is bypassed. If substantial sales are to be realized, of course, authors still have to figure out how to promote their products to a mass market.

Comedy writers can now submit material for electronic publication, which is read on a laptop, handheld reader, or other device.

AGENTS AND PUBLISHERS

Even if you self-publish, chances are you won't hit the "big time" without an agent or a mainstream publisher. You might reach a certain level of success on your own (via self-publishing, print on demand, or e-book publishing). But you won't reach the upper stratosphere of publishing success without the knowledge, power, and "muscle" that a publisher and established literary agent provide.

When agent-hunting, is it best to wear orange or camouflage?

Help required

Self-publishing might be empowering or instill a sense of accomplishment. It may be therapeutic to be proactive. And some sales—even meager ones—might be self-affirming and even pay a few bills. But you are essentially doing those things to capture the attention of a major literary agent or publisher. No one reaches number one on the best seller list alone.

Agent-hunting

The traditional route—hunting for an agent, manuscript in hand, sorting through piles of disheartening rejection letters—is still an option (and probably the most popular). Plenty of books and articles spell out that process in detail. Agents and publishers have a pretty good presence online and their web sites outline their requirements at length. Spend time researching these, as it will prevent you wasting time down the line.

STEFANIE WILDER-TAYLOR

Stefanie is author of *Sippy Cups are not for Chardonnay, and Other Things I Had to Learn as a New Mom* and *Naptime is the New Happy Hour, and Other Ways Toddlers Turn Your Life Upside Down*. Both were based on her prominent blog "Baby on Bored," which has been entertaining thousands of mothers since 2005. She is the humorous parenting guru on NBC's *The Today Show*, and has also appeared on *Oprah, Dr. Phil, Larry King Live,* and *Real Savvy Moms* (on PBS). She has performed on *Make Me Laugh, Evening at the Improv,* and at the Montreal Comedy Festival. *It's Not Me, It's You: Subjective Recollections of a Terminally Optimistic, Chronically Sarcastic, and Occasionally Inebriated Woman* is her third book, and a fourth, *I'm Kind of a Big Deal*, is on its way. Stefanie hasn't slowed down, despite her three young children!

do consider myself a recovering standup comic, turned blogger, turned author. I never did love doing the actual standup, I mostly liked writing the jokes and then finding out they were funny ... I decided to concentrate on starting a blog just to get the funny out before it was all sucked out of my breast by my baby. After I started the blog, I sent it to my friends who get my humor and one of them sent it to their agent and that agent got me a book deal. Only in Hollywood, right?

Stefanie Wilder-Taylor

MAGAZINES

When we think of magazines, we envisage *Paris Match, Der Spiegel, or Vanity Fair,* right? Of course, having your humor published in one of these publications is a laudable goal, but in the meantime, there are literally thousands of magazines that cater to specialized audiences and industries. For every *Time,* there are a dozen *World War II Re-Enactors* magazines.

SMALL PRINT

Take a gander inside the magazine itself to find out how to submit. The publisher's address is often in the back of the magazine—sometimes on the very last page, inside the back cover. At the very bottom, there will frequently be a small paragraph in italics that spells out what they're looking for, how to submit material, and how much they pay!

While most magazine copy is generated "in-house," many publications seek and publish material from freelancers.

WRITER'S MARKET

If you can't get your hands on all the thousands of magazines that are published in this world—or if you've been kicked out of the local bookstore for peeking inside each and every copy of its magazine collection—you can still pick up *Writer's Market*, which contains listings for 3,500 magazines, periodicals, monthlies, weeklies, and annuals. (You also get a free subscription to its online version, which contains another 2,500 listings.) A surprising number of publications want funny articles, short-form humor, gags, jokes, or images, and you will be able to find detailed information about thousands of magazines. In some cases, you can discover—direct from the editors themselves—how and when to send in your comedic jewels, how much they pay … even how long it takes them to send you your check!

Private Eye magazine is the U.K.'s foremost political comedy magazine. It features in-depth editorial as well as slapstick-style captions and lighthearted analysis.

Chuckle-churner?

Everyone has heard of *Rolling Stone*, but how many are familiar with *Elevator World*? It is startling enough to learn that these magazines exist, but it's even more fascinating that a good number of them have the occasional need for humorous content. It is an immutable law in publishing that a magazine shall give its readers at least one or two chuckles per issue. Many of them solicit this material from outside sources, and you could be one of them.

BLOG

The medium of choice for many humorists is the "blog" (short for "weblog," a log that is published on the Internet). A blog is a web site that uses so-called blog technology and enables the user to easily publish timely content (text, pictures, videos, links, etc.) in dated, chronological order. It costs nothing to set up a blog. You have complete control over the content—you can even opt to make it private. Your blog can cover one topic, a handful of topics, or it can encompass the entire universe. You can update it as often, or as seldom, as you like. Your blog "posts" can be short, or long, or in between.

To paraphrase the old saying, "Blog about what you know."

Why blog?

Writing a blog can be an ideal way to sharpen your writing skills. It keeps you thinking creatively, and it is a useful means of getting feedback on your writing. Blogs are ideal showcases for your comic musings. If you promote your blog via networking and other means, you can grow your readership (or develop a "fanbase," if you prefer). Blogging can lead to other opportunities, as well—online or offline.

Blogging can be done from home, on your own schedule, wearing your pajamas.

WILL BLOG FOR WORK

Sometimes a creative outlet can lead to a paying gig. Sean Medlock, aka "Jim Treacher," blogs as the "DC Trawler" for the Daily Caller, Tucker Carlson's Washington, D.C.-based 24-hour news site. He explains how he got the gig.

"I STARTED BLOGGING SHORTLY AFTER 9/11. THAT SEEMED TO BE THE CATALYST FOR A LOT OF BLOGGERS. I STARTED E-MAILING LINKS AND COMMENTS TO VARIOUS BLOGS, UNTIL IT OCCURRED TO ME THAT IT WOULD BE EASIER JUST TO START MY OWN. 'HEY, ALL THESE OTHER GUYS ARE DOING IT. WHY NOT?' THERE WAS NOBODY TELLING ME NOT TO. WELL, NOBODY WORTH LISTENING TO … THE 'JIM TREACHER' THING WAS A MESSAGE-BOARD PSEUDONYM, WHICH I USED SO MY THEN-EMPLOYER WOULDN'T KNOW I WAS SCREWING AROUND ON THE JOB. EVEN AFTER I GOT LAID OFF IN APRIL '01, I CONTINUED TO USE THAT PEN NAME AND IT JUST SORT OF STUCK. THESE DAYS, I WISH I'D TAKEN A LITTLE TIME AND THOUGHT OF A BETTER ONE. 'BUSTER HYMEN,' PERHAPS, OR MAYBE 'I. P. FREELY.' SOMETHING WITH A LITTLE MORE DIGNITY. SO I STARTED A BLOG AND JUST WROTE WHATEVER I FELT LIKE, AND I MANAGED TO BUILD A SMALL AUDIENCE. EIGHT SHORT YEARS LATER, AN INSANE TV PUNDIT ASKED ME TO ACCEPT A LIVING WAGE FOR DOING THE SAME THING. SO FAR HE HAS NOT REALIZED HIS ENORMOUS MISTAKE."

SEAN MEDLOCK

YOUTUBE

YouTube launched in 2005. It's a web site that enables people to upload and view music videos, TV, and movie clips, quickly and easily, using Adobe Flash technology. It is a major factor in the explosion of "user-generated content." YouTube has already birthed many mass-market successes.

Video-sharing web sites offer more than just cats playing the piano. Often you can see dogs playing the piano!

TEEN DREAM

Bo Burnham was a 16-year-old high school student who wrote, performed, and videotaped a handful of politically incorrect songs about being a teenager. He uploaded the videos to YouTube for friends and relatives to watch. Just over one year later, he taped a live performance in London which aired on *Comedy Central*, and then signed a four-record deal with that network's record label. Burnham is in demand as a live performer, he starred in a one-hour special for *Comedy Central*, and is involved in major studio movie and television production projects.

BROOKERS

In September 2005, Brooke Brodack started uploading her humorous videos to her YouTube channel. She had shot several such videos in her bedroom and around her house. These were parodies of other popular videos or spoofs of movies or television. Mere months later, she signed an 18-month development deal with NBC.

A video becomes "viral" when the video's link is passed among friends, family, and co-workers, via e-mail or social networking sites.

> 'm really busted up over this and I'm very, very sorry to those people in the audience, the blacks, the Hispanics, whites—everyone that was there that took the brunt of that anger and hate and rage and how it came through.

Michael Richards, after his "racist rant" became an Internet sensation

10
CONTACTS AND QUESTIONS

Dean Martin once jokingly said, "Milton Berle is an inspiration to every young person that wants to get into show business. Hard work, perseverance, and discipline: all the things you need … when you have no talent." Of course, hard work, perseverance, and discipline are all the things you need—even if you have talent oozing out of your pores. A career in show business doesn't just happen. Somebody has to *make* it happen. People who achieve notoriety through happenstance still need hard work, perseverance, and discipline to remain in the public eye. There is a business side to the show. It's as important—some might argue that it is more important—as the show itself.

MARKETING

Famed prop comic and actor Carrot Top has admitted in countless interviews, "I had a logo before I even had an act." He is one of the few comics who had a fundamental understanding of the importance of marketing, from very early on in his career, as he graduated with a Marketing degree from Florida Atlantic University. But, of course, he also worked hard on his material.

Basic skills

Without the ability to perform, marketing is like advertising an inferior product or one that doesn't exist. While some comics and actors do have more talent for marketing than others, there are still some basic (pretty much mandatory) skills that a comedian must acquire. If you can't do it yourself, pull out the credit card and find somebody who can do it for you.

Audition tape

The idea of an audition "tape" is a misnomer. Magnetic tape will disappear in our lifetimes, but the terminology persists, and people will say "Send me a tape" when they're really referring to a DVD (though even they may soon disappear). There will come a time—in the not-too-distant future—when the idea of sending a physical object of any kind will vanish. An audition "tape" generally refers to a videotaped performance, typically using a digital camera, and sent via electronic mail—it may be your most important means of getting work. Some folks require a tape even before setting up a live audition, so while it's not necessary to spend thousands of dollars recording your set it should look as professional as possible. An inexpensive digital recorder can be set up—on either a tripod or just a tabletop—that will deliver a usable-quality video. And, though there isn't any tape involved, it's still generally referred to as "taping." Make sure the sound is good: try to eliminate ambient noise or audience chatter. The camera

WHICH FORMAT?

It's best to have your audition tape in two formats—burned onto a DVD or uploaded to an online hosting service (YouTube or similar web site). Some people might require a physical DVD (sent via conventional mail), while others need only a link to an online audition video (via e-mail).

> "I AM THE BOSS. IT ISN'T JUST THE MARKETING. EVERYONE WORKS FOR ME. MY MANAGER WORKS FOR ME. YOU GOT THE SOUND GUY WORKING FOR YOU, THE LIGHT GUY WORKING FOR YOU, THE STAGE GUYS WORK FOR YOU, YOU GOT THREE ASSISTANTS DOWN THERE AND WARDROBE."
>
> GEORGE WALLACE

An audition tape must be in front of a crowd, in a performance venue, not in your basement or outdoors or via a webcam while sitting at your computer.

needs to be zoomed in as tightly as possible on the performer (you!), and a "waist-up" shot is preferable. Five to ten minutes is the maximum length most people will view, but it's always good to have a longer set available—be prepared for any eventuality. Some club owners or bookers claim to be able to make a judgment based on just 10 minutes; others will want to see more—for example, some leave nothing to chance, requiring a 30-minute set to approve a comic for a 30-minute club slot.

The headshot

Headshots (better known as "8 x 10s") may not be as important to comics as they are to actors, but are still necessary. Not only does it make you look like a professional performer, but it also helps club managers, club owners, and agents in promoting shows. A headshot should be well-lit, sharply focused, with good contrast. It can also be a three-quarter or full-body shot.

BRIAN McKIM

Unlike an acting headshot, a comedy headshot can be whimsical, slightly offbeat, or involve props.

TRACI SKENE

Digital rules

With the explosion of digital photography (almost totally supplanting traditional analog photography), headshots are now expected to be in color. And, since digital photographs can be stored and easily sent via the Internet, it is important that a copy of the headshot, usually in a high-resolution, JPEG format, be hosted somewhere online. This enables you to easily send a headshot via electronic mail or invite someone to download such a file via the Internet.

Bio tips

A bio should never be more than one page when printed. A good way to make sure your bio is never over this limit is to compose it, then save it as a PDF file—which is easily viewed and printed using the popular, free Adobe Acrobat Reader software. There is readily available, inexpensive (and often free) software that can help you create a PDF.

Composing your bio

You need to compose a short written "bio" of yourself and your act. Unlike a résumé, which merely states your experience and skills, a bio should be breezier and more interesting. You can take a little license with a bio and inject some of your sensibilities into it. Here's a sample bio from Brian Regan:

Critics and peers agree, Brian Regan has distinguished himself as one of the premier comedians in the country. The perfect balance of sophisticated writing and physicality, Brian fills theaters nationwide with fervent fans that span generations. Releasing two critically acclaimed hour Comedy Central specials and DVDs in as many years, 2008's The Epitome of Hyperbole and 2007's Brian Regan Standing Up, Brian has set a standard of excellence that others continually try to follow. Brian's nonstop theater tour has visited more than 80 cities each year since 2005 and continues into 2009. It is the quality of his material, relatable to a wide audience and revered by his peers, which continues to grow Brian's fan base. With his first appearance on The Late Show with David Letterman in 1995, Brian solidified his place on the show and recently made his 20th appearance. He also includes regular visits to Late Night with Conan O'Brien on his schedule. A dorm room favorite, Brian's 1997 CD, Brian Regan Live, has sold over 150,000 copies and consistently charts in iTunes Top Ten Comedy Albums. Brian's 2000 Comedy Central Presents special continues to be a top viewer choice and Brian's independently released 2004 DVD, I Walked on the Moon, is available at www.brianregan.com.

Fan clubs

In the past, sports figures, musical acts, and comedians formed "fan clubs," which answered letters, sent out newsletters and autographed memorabilia, and promoted live appearances. They were usually run by an individual (a trusted friend or associate), organized and executed by a fan, or, in some cases, run by a firm specializing in publicity or public relations. Often record labels or movie studios ran them as an adjunct to a general publicity plan. Web sites and social media make it possible for performers to interact directly—and at little cost—with fans.

If you tell a fan to go away and he or she doesn't go away ... you've got yourself a stalker.

The Undisputed Heavyweight Social
Media Champion of the World:
Dane Cook!

DANE COOK

In 2002, Dane spent his
$25,000 savings on a web
site—danecook.com—using it to
promote his burgeoning career.
Cook was an early adapter of
myspace.com, the site that enables
people to meet new friends, keep in
touch with old ones, and recommend
music or movies. Cook soon had 2.8
million Myspace "friends" and used
the site to communicate with fans and
promote upcoming live dates, television
appearances, CD releases, and other
projects. Cook had 1.6 million
followers on Twitter at last count
and 3.6 million fans via Facebook.

(Online) press kits

Press kits are used to get bookings or
attract the attention of representation or
the press, often including a headshot, bio,
audition tape, business card, and a few
press clippings. Online or electronic press
kits (EPKs) are fast supplanting the physical
version (which can be mailed or hand-
delivered) as the method of promotion.
They are infinitely changeable, incurring
no additional printing costs, and can link to
any number of articles. With creativity and
care, they can be pleasant, entertaining
experiences in their own right, containing
audio, video, stills, and text. Everything
on an EPK should be downloadable.
Headshots should be high resolution—

usable for online reproduction or printing
in newspapers, magazines, or on photo
paper. Audio clips must be usable for radio
promotion—crisp, clear and, depending
on where you want them to air, free of
profanity. Video clips (such as those
hosted on YouTube) should have an embed
code so clubs can easily include them on
their web sites.

FACEBOOK

A Facebook page or fan page can
be an inexpensive substitute for a
web site. It can also offer a means
of communicating with bookers, fans,
and others.

iTunes

If you have a clear, stereo audio recording of your set (to which you own the rights), you can distribute your comedy recordings through Apple's software-based online digital media store iTunes. Apply through the web site's iTunes Connect. If you are approved, you will be able to sell individual tracks or an entire CD of your comedy via digital downloading.

Satellite radio

You can also send a CD copy of your material to Sirius XM, the satellite radio service. It has an appetite for comedy material, as it programs several "stations" that broadcast mostly recordings of live standup and song parodies

Other services

Soundexchange, a nonprofit performance rights organization, collects royalties on behalf of comics, musicians, and others whose music or comedy are played on various satellite services. Sign up with Soundexchange, and they'll track the number of plays and cut you a check on a quarterly basis. A similar outfit, Comedy Exchange Association, exists to perform the same service with regard to comedy recordings played on terrestrial radio.

Kathleen Madigan's recordings are consistently among the top iTunes comedy album downloads.

don't do any of my old stuff ... It's just
o weird to do jokes that people already
now the end to. Friends of mine, peers,
ill sometimes do an encore with old
tuff, and let people yell out the end.
But for me, it's boring, so I don't want to
do it, and also, I don't remember a lot of
hose jokes. You record them and they live
orever, but to be honest, I couldn't get
through half those jokes. So I just do what
I want, regardless. I don't worry too much
about that stuff. If they want to see those
jokes, they can steal them off the Internet
like normal people. I mean everything's
on YouTube, so I don't need to hawk it
or retell it.

Daniel Tosh

PROS AND CONS OF AGENTS

The primary goal of an agent is to get you work. Don't seek out the services of an agent until you are ready to make both of you some money. More often than not, an agent will find you. The best way to find an agent is to put yourself in the proximity of agents—by performing in major entertainment capitals (Los Angeles, New York, Sydney, Melbourne, London, Paris, etc.) or by entering contests or festivals. Networking with other comedians can also provide the necessary introduction or recommendation that can lead to representation. Some experienced comics have more than one agent— one for live performance, maybe, or one for acting, or commercials or for voiceover bookings. Others just let one agency handle all of their needs.

A good agent will allow you to pay more attention to the "show" and less attention to the "business."

The difference between a 'manager' and an 'agent' is right there in the title. One helps you manage your career while keeping an eye focused way down the road at some particular goal. (Acting, HBO special, opening a club.) And the other creates a reaction for you. (Gets bookers interested in using you, gets you meetings with TV execs, etc.) Whereas a good manager is always thinking of how decisions now help you get down the road to your long-term goals, a good agent is focused on getting you work, any work, right now, this week. I believe that your act dictates when it's time to look into some sort of representation. As a local act you can field all the calls yourself. You can send out your avails to some of the nearby clubs and that's fine. But when the amount of time you spend self-promoting and dealing with bookers starts to outweigh the time and focus you spend working on the act—that is the time to look into landing a manager. A good manager is someone just as focused on your career as you. He or she should know your long-term goals and should always be thinking of ways to move you toward those goals. Together you can make decisions that move you beyond the local market and into being a regional act and, in time, a national act. It is my experience that working relationships with managers are usually long, long relationships. Whereas talent jumps agencies constantly—so do agents for that matter. Management is about the long haul. Agents are about the immediate procurement of work. Agents usually have more power in getting you work because they have something that most managers don't: a roster. A club booker could talk to a few managers in a week and fill a few dates for the club or he or she could make one phone call to an agency and fill half a calendar year. That is not to say you and your manager couldn't get you work. My point is, from the club's point of view, dealing with an agency is more efficient.

JOE STARR has appeared at the Just For Laughs Festival in Montreal and is featured in the Steven Spielberg-directed *The Adventures of Tintin: Secret of the Unicorn*

Does your manager have a reputation for being trustworthy? It's easy enough to find out: Ask around.

Managers

The relationship with your manager tends to be a bit more personal, so your manager should be someone you trust. If the person you choose doesn't have complete faith in your talent or abilities, find another manager! Not only can a good manager help you realize your career goals, but he or she can also help you find a good agent.

> "YOU SHOULD TRUST YOUR MANAGER ENOUGH TO BELIEVE HE ISN'T THE REASON YOU ARE FAILING AND, IF HE IS, GET A NEW ONE. OF COURSE MANAGEMENT HELPS. IT'S NECESSARY. THAT'S THE WAY THE BUSINESS IS SET UP. YOU SHOULD LIKE YOUR MANAGER BUT HE IS NOT YOUR FRIEND. HE IS A BUSINESS PARTNER."
>
> MARC MARON

ENTERTAINMENT LAWYER OR BUSINESS MANAGER

Some comics manage to have a successful career without the assistance of a manager or an agent. However, if you choose that route, it's a good idea to retain the services of a good entertainment lawyer to look after your interests. Such attorneys are familiar with the ins and outs of entertainment law—contracts, royalties, syndication—and can be a great help when making important decisions. Business managers are similar, and quite often double up as attorneys.

ROCKY'S MICKEY

There's a famous scene in *Rocky*, where Burgess Meredith as trainer Mickey Goldmill confronts Sylvester Stallone's Rocky Balboa: "What you need," Goldmill growls, "is a MANAGER." His point is that talent, hard work, and perseverance can only get you so far. At some point, you will need a manager.

The pitfalls of representation

Large agencies and management companies have power and connections that are unrivaled. But they also have a lot of clients. As such, there's a danger that you might be overlooked—or even be ignored—by the very people who claim to represent you. Smaller agencies might give you more personalized attention, but they also don't have as much clout as the big boys. So, it's a tradeoff. Tough decision, and one you should think about very carefully. It's also important to read the contract before you sign it. A small amount of money paid to an attorney now can save you a lot of time and all sorts of heartache down the road.

Initially just a goof, The Blues Brothers were never supposed to go anywhere. The band's guitarist called it a "happy accident" when the act exploded.

TV SET

Getting ready for a television set requires a lot of preparation. Doing a 4:30 set on a late-night talk show is very different from crafting a set of a similar length for a live comedy club performance. Parameters vary from show to show, and television in general has peculiar quirks and limitations.

COPING WITH FAME

Nothing can prepare you for fame. Not a book, nor a movie, nor a class, nor even proximity to a famous person, can help you fully grasp what it must be like to lose your anonymity. At first, signing autographs can be fun, and posing for pictures is flattering. Being recognized on the street is downright exhilarating.

Nice on the way up

Being followed by paparazzi or mobbed at the store by fans can be overwhelming. It's no wonder some people—even people who have been in the business for years—suddenly can't handle being thrust into the spotlight. Ironically, losing that fame once you've become accustomed to it can often be worse. Your best bet is to be nice on the way up. It'll help you once you get up there and will be even more of a help should you find yourself on the way down.

Television

The most powerful mass medium ever devised, television has unrivaled power to reach millions of people. It goes without saying that you should make every effort to prepare yourself to eventually appear on television. Performing for television is

From time to time, you may wonder, "What have I gotten myself into?"

a different beast altogether from live performance. There are often restrictions on time, language, or dress, for example.

Getting a slot

The number of slots for comedians on late-night talk shows, panel shows, weekly variety shows, or specials is necessarily limited. Getting one of those slots will not be easy. What is easy, however, is obtaining the information on how to secure such a slot. Call the network that produces the show you're interested in. Ask for contact information for the talent coordinator for that show. Contact him or her, asking what is required. Or call the company that produces that show and find out what is required. Or ask someone who has appeared on a show just how to go about approaching the appropriate network, cable outlet, or production company. Alternatively, if you encounter someone who works for the show in question, ask him or her for the pertinent information.

WEB SITES AND FESTIVALS

A festival is a good place to hop onto The Wheel of Fame and Fortune.

Web sites about comedy

There are several web sites that cater to comedians and fans of comedy, offering news and opinions about standup comedy. Some of the more popular web sites are:

punchlinemagazine.com
Started in 2006, reviews U.S. standup comedy films, DVDs, and specials.

sheckymagazine.com
The authors' web site, established in 1999.

www.comedyeurope.com
Covers comedy in Europe.

nuttybeaver.com
Covers comedy in Canada.

www.chortle.co.uk
Covers comedy in the U.K.

au.chortle.com
The Australia and New Zealand version of Chortle.

Festivals

There are a handful of major annual comedy festivals throughout the world, featuring comedians from around the planet, offering exposure for those who are invited to perform, and networking opportunities for industry executives, agents, managers, and media.

Just For Laughs

www.hahaha.com

Takes place in Montreal, QC, Canada, in July. The first portion features French-language performances and street performers. The second portion features comedians from around the world.

Cat Laughs Comedy Festival

www.thecatlaughs.com

Founded in 1994, "in response to the burgeoning wealth of Irish comic talent with no clear national outlet for expression." Takes place in June.

Edinburgh Festival Fringe

www.edfringe.com

The Edinburgh Festival Fringe is the largest arts festival in the world, and takes place every August for three weeks in Scotland's capital city.

Melbourne International Comedy Festival

www.comedyfestival.com.au

Takes place in Melbourne every April.

There are numerous other festivals varying in size and influence, in cities throughout the world—in locations like Calgary, Boston, Hong Kong, Chicago, Toronto, Miami, Detroit, and many more. If you aspire to perform in a festival, it's a great idea to attend one beforehand, so you can get a feel for the festival experience. Performing in a major festival can provide a major boost to a comedy career.

GLOSSARY

Agent: A person who acts as a liaison between you and a television or movie studio, or between you and a comedy club or theater. He or she understands the business and can negotiate favorable terms for your employment.

Alternative comedy: This means two different things, depending on which side of the Atlantic you're on. In America, the alternative comedy scene sprouted in Los Angeles and New York as a reaction to what was perceived as a stagnation of comedy during the "comedy boom." The comedy boom in America started in the late- to mid-1970s, gaining steam in 1982 and lasting until 1992. It was a period of great growth in the comedy club business and marked by an explosion of professional comedians and a profusion of standup comedy on cable and network television. Prior to the comedy boom, there were a relatively small number of professional comedians and relatively few venues nationwide for comedians to perform in (virtually none solely dedicated to standup). It was thought by the alternative comedians (and their agents and managers) that standup was in need of a fresh approach. With increasing frequency, starting roughly in 1990 or so, unconventional venues offered alternative standup comedy nights and some clubs specialized in alternative standup. Before long, the "alt-movement" had recognizable "stars" who went on to success in television, movies, and live standup performance.

In the U.K. in the early 1970s, the comedy scene was much like the U.S. scene. A relatively small number of professional comedians performing in working men's clubs, music halls, theaters, and a handful achieving success on television and in movies. At roughly the same time as the comedy boom was occurring in the U.S., the U.K. saw the opening of comedy clubs—that is, venues dedicated exclusively to presenting standup comedy. Their "alternative" comedians were similar in sensibilities and style to the crop of comedians that presaged the U.S. comedy boom.

Blog: Short for "weblog." A blog is an ingenious technology that enables a writer to publish his or her thoughts, catalog them, have them displayed on a web site in chronological order, and invite comment from readers around the world. It is ideal for an aspiring comedian or comedy writer who wants to sharpen his or her comedy writing skills and/or demonstrate an ability to regularly produce high-quality comedy.

Bombing, to bomb: When you perform and get little or no reaction from the audience ... or an outright hostile reaction. It can also be said that you "died" or "ate it."

Character comedian: A comedian who always—in every performance—assumes an obvious character onstage, often using a pseudonym. Famous examples would be "Larry The Cable Guy," "Charlie Weaver," "Minnie Pearl," "Peewee Herman," or "Dame Edna." It is a prime example of P.O.V. (see page 248) taken to an absurd extreme. Nearly every comic assumes a character onstage, but the character comedian broadens it and brings it front and center.

Context: The setting or circumstances in which comedy is performed. Context is often a consideration when choosing material. It doesn't refer to the venue (although the venue certainly might figure into one's assessment of context). It refers to somewhat finer details, which can sometimes dictate whether or not a joke or a topic is "appropriate." To be sure, there are venues/situations where it is understood that "anything goes." But there are a multitude of other situations where one might consider the context before using certain language or broaching certain topics. It is advisable to determine what, if any, limitations on free expression exist before performing and to make any adjustments that might be necessary ... or, just do what you want and deal with the consequences.

Crowd work: The act of talking with an audience member (or multiple audience members) in the course of your act, often, it is hoped, with hilarious results. Also known as "going into the crowd." It takes considerable skill to "work the crowd," since it is a form of improvisation and it also risks giving up some control of the situation. While it is true that audience members will frequently respond in a predictable fashion (especially to carefully constructed questions), crowd work takes nerves of steel, confidence in one's innate sense of humor, and an ability to "read" an audience and to know when to withdraw.

D.I.Y.: An abbreviation for "do it yourself." With modern technology being what it is, it is quite often easier to just do it yourself. "It" can be any of a number of things that, in the past, you had to ask someone else to do … and you had to pay that someone else a small fortune to do it. Nowadays, the D.I.Y. spirit has empowered performers and entertainers and cut out any number of middlemen up and down the line—this is known as "disintermediation" (see page 219).

Hack: A shortening of the word "hackneyed," which is a word meaning "lacking in freshness or originality." It is, as you can imagine, a pejorative term. It can be an adjective used to describe a comedian or a comedian's material. It can be also be a noun used to describe the comedian who is adjudged to have used hack material. NOTE: Some modern comedians use the term, rather confusingly, interchangeably with "steal." This is in limited use.

Heckler: An audience member who engages in "heckling," which is an attempt by various means to disrupt the comedy performance. He or she may utilize any of a number of tactics to unnerve or distract the performer. It is unclear as to why the heckler heckles. To gain attention? Out of deep-seated jealousy? An utter failure to grasp certain bedrock social conventions? It is up to the performer to regain control by any means necessary should the venue not see fit to eject the heckler. Fortunately heckling is rare. Rare though it may be, it is unsettling. It is best to be prepared.

Hook: A word or a catchphrase that ties together a comedian's act thematically. It can take many forms, and it can serve many purposes. It can tie together seemingly disparate elements in a comic's presentation. It can give audience members a compact, easily remembered phrase or sentiment that in turn makes the comedian easy to remember. Often a hook will give a comic a central theme to write around.

Killing, to kill: The act of performing standup successfully. If the entire room is laughing (and laughing hard) for most or all of your set, it can be said that you killed. It can also be said that you "crushed," or "destroyed."

The light: A light, usually red, usually at the center and rear of the venue, that is switched on to indicate that it is time for the performer to "wrap it up" (prepare to get off stage). Often, a comic can ask for a "one-minute light," which is a light to indicate that he or she has one minute to bring the act to a close. Failure to adhere to this convention will result in shunning … or worse.

Manager: A person who understands the entertainment business and can guide you in your quest to forge a career in show business. He or she can, with input from you, determine how best to go about achieving your goals.

Material: A term that is often interchangeable with "jokes." A comedian's material is the sum total of all the humor—the jokes, the anecdotes, song parodies, etc.—that he or she has written and performed and honed. When buying and selling jokes, the commodity is often referred to as material.

One-liner: A joke that is concise, to the point, and usually only one sentence long. It is essentially a setup and a punch line incorporated into one line. One-liners are a specialized form of standup. And the "one-liner comics" who employ them—most notably Henny Youngman, Steve Wright, Mitch Hedberg, Jimmy Carr—must produce reams of material, since each joke takes up far less time onstage than, say, a lengthy anecdote.

Open mic (also "open mike"): Short for "open microphone," this is a show that affords amateurs or novices the opportunity to perform in front of a live audience and learn "on the job." There is often a "sign-up" during which the names of hopefuls are collected, after which a slot on the bill is assigned. There is usually no pay. Often musical or variety acts will perform.

Opener/MC, Middle/Feature, Closer/Headliner: The three positions on a three-person comedy show. The opener is obviously the first act. Quite often he or she will be the MC (Master of Ceremonies). The MC, in most situations, will come out first, "warm up" the crowd, do a short set, and then bring on the next (or "middle" or "feature") act. Often the MC will then be expected to re-take the stage after the middle set and prepare the audience for the closing or final act of the evening. It is expected that the MC will memorize (or attempt to memorize) the introductions of the other acts and deliver said introductions with enthusiasm. The MC is the second most important act on the bill—the most important being the act that goes on last. The preceding describes a typical scenario but is by no means standard. Various markets and countries have different ways of configuring shows. As far as the amount of time each act does, it is common for the MC to do a short set and for the closing act to do a lengthy set. The feature act often will be called upon to do a set that is somewhere in between. Aspiring comedians who wish to garner stage time would do well to master the art of emceeing, since few comedians relish the task of hosting a show.

Packet: In sketch writing, a packet consists of several scripts for sketches that clearly demonstrate your ability to imagine scenarios, premises, and full scenes which can be realized by a troupe of sketch artists or actors. Having such a packet—and being able to send it along to agents, producers, or show runners—is important if you wish to be hired as a sketch writer on a television show, or by an improv theater.

Persona: Similar to P.O.V., but more related to the physical quirks, tics, or mannerisms of the performer. Voice, dress, hand gestures, and movement—all taken together make up the comedian's persona.

Pilot script: A script for the first episode of a new sitcom or television series. The pilot episode is intended to test audience reaction and to judge whether the series will be successful.

P.O.V. (or POV): This stands for "point of view," and refers to the overarching theme of your onstage presentation (act, routine, or set). Your P.O.V. makes your act seem coherent. It gives the audience something to grab onto, a way to relate to you and your material. It provides context for all of your observations. And, conversely, your P.O.V. can give you a framework for writing and a direction to take your material in. A strong, coherent P.O.V. is allegedly what television producers look for when they seek out comedians upon which to build a sitcom. If you lack a defined P.O.V., it can be hard for an audience to get to "know" you.

Premise: The idea that a joke is based upon. A premise is not a joke, but is merely the foundation for a joke. Merely cooking up a bunch of premises does not make for a night of hilarity. The premise must be "developed" into a joke. To put it another way, you may, through your mighty powers of observation, discover many seemingly paradoxical or contradictory or perhaps merely interesting situations or conditions as you go about your daily life— my cat likes to sleep in the spot of sun on my living room floor, my car fails to start when I have somewhere really important to go, or my significant other claims to love me but does the most horrible things to me. None of these observations by themselves are jokes. They must be "fleshed out" in order to evoke laughter.

Punch line: The part of your joke or story that gets the biggest response (laughter, it is hoped). Preferably at the end of the joke. It

is the joke's reason for being. If it doesn't get a laugh, it can't very well be called a punch line (see Setup, below). If there are shorter, concise statements after the main punch line, they are called "taglines" or simply "tags."

Rim shot: The sound played by a drummer to augment or enhance a comedian's punch line. It's not done much any more. It's mainly a holdover from the mid-twentieth century, so it's not employed much, except by older comedians. But if you hear it, you now know what it's called.

Rule of threes: An odd "law" or "rule" that says that things are funnier when grouped in threes. Specifically in a punch line. No one seems to know why, but if you create and deliver a punch line and the end of the punch line involves, say, a list of items, it is best to list three items, the third one of which should be the real or true punch line. Hard to explain, but trust us, you'll see that three is better than two or four.

Satire: This is humor that seeks to ridicule human vice or folly. More often than not, satire is social or political in nature, targeting the famous or the powerful— politicians, industrialists, or celebrities. It can be sketch comedy, film, musical parody, standup, written essays, plays—any form of humor. Satire employs sarcasm, wit, and often a bit of an edge. Satire without an edge is … whining.

Set: That collection of jokes, songs, anecdotes, improvisation, or crowd interaction that makes up a comedian's performance. A set can vary in length, depending on the requirements of the situation. An open-mic comedian might do a five-minute set. An accomplished headliner may do a set that lasts an hour or more. A "set list" is a list, often hand-written, that enumerates all the jokes that a comedian intends to include in a set. Often, for practicality, it will merely contain "bullet points" or key words, as opposed to entire jokes. Occasionally, it will merely contain topics that the comedian wishes to touch upon in an effort to "work out" material. In rare instances, it is referred to as a "cheat sheet," though few people believe that having a list to facilitate recall is "cheating" in any sense of the word.

Setup: The part of the joke that prefaces the punch line. It prepares the audience by giving them information, setting a scene, outlining a premise, etc. In rare cases, the setup itself will get a laugh, but such is not preferable. In psychological terms, the setup creates tension, which is relieved by the punch line.

Show bible: A reference document used by scriptwriters for information on a story's characters and settings, and to keep track of details. It is commonly used in media with multiple writers, such as sitcoms and television series, to ensure continuity with previous episodes.

Sketch comedy: Usually done with two or more people and usually planned out either using a loose framework of scenarios and beats or totally scripted down to the last word. Sketches are scenes or scenarios played out in discrete chunks, with a beginning, a

middle, and an end. Sketch comedy can be political or social satire, it can be absurdist, it can be zany, or it can incorporate any or all of these elements.

Spec script: A script written "on spec" ("spec" being short for "speculation" or "speculative") is intended not as a "working" or "shooting" script but merely as a sample of the author's writing, and a way to demonstrate that the author understands (and can successfully execute) the conventions of script writing. A spec script can be for a movie or a television show. It is best to have a spec script or two at the ready, just in case anyone asks you if you know how to write a script.

Stealing: Intentionally performing material or jokes that you didn't write or purchase. On rare occasions, comedians will concoct a joke that is identical to that of another comedian. It is said that in such cases, no stealing has taken place, but that it is a case of "parallel development." As you might imagine, comedians take a dim view of stealing. If you can't do original comedy, it is strongly suggested that you pursue another line of work.

Story arc: An extended or continuing story line in a sitcom or television series, which unfolds over many episodes.

Timing: It is said that timing is a necessary skill for a comedian. It is an innate sense of how fast or how slow to tell a joke, when to slow down or speed up to maximize the impact of the words in the sentence, when to rein in the act in general, or when to fire on all

cylinders. In music, it is akin to a musician's feel for tempo, rhythm, and meter, but is infinitely harder to explain. Or teach. If you don't have timing, you probably can't learn it.

Variety act: A performer who eschews the standard format of a lone man or woman, standing on the stage telling jokes/stories. Variety acts include, but are not limited to, clowns, "guitar acts," mimes, jugglers, magicians, prop acts, impressionists, comics who use audio/visual presentations, or ventriloquists.

Wordplay: Jokes involving words—similarity between words, confusion with words, the sound of the word, etc.—are often referred to as "wordplay." For example, a pun: "My optometrist is so egotistical. Everything is 'Eye! Eye! Eye!'" Of course, the optometrist is not at all egotistical, for the speaker has confused "I" with "eye." Puns and wordplay often elicit groans rather than outright laughs, but they can form the basis for good, solid jokes.

Writer's Market: A publication (and a companion web site) that offers purchasers/subscribers information on the many publications, people, and companies that offer money in return for humor—usually written, hence the name! If you aspire to churn out humor but don't know where to peddle it, the Writer's Market may be what you're looking for.

INDEX

ACKNOWLEDGMENTS

We'd like to thank Shecky Greene, "the funniest natural comedian ever to play Las Vegas," for "lending" us his name when we started our blog in 1999. And thanks go to Martha Burley and Ruth Patrick for their guidance during this process. And, of course, we thank all the comics we've laughed with in green rooms, diners, cars, and bars.

All interview quotes in this book have been collated from a variety of sources. Quintet has made every effort to avoid misquotations, but would be happy to correct any issues on future reprints.

PICTURE CREDITS

All other images are the copyright of Quintet Publishing Ltd. While every effort has been made to credit contributors, Quintet Publishing would like to apologize should there have been any omissions or errors— and would be pleased to make the appropriate correction for future editions of the book.

Alamy: 9 © Trinity Mirror / Mirrorpix / Alamy; 10 © Craig Holmes / Alamy; 11 © Trinity Mirror / Mirrorpix / Alamy; 21 © Photos 12 / Alamy; 23 © Linda Matlow/PIXINTL / Alamy; 25 © Alamy / Alamy; 27 © Pictorial Press Ltd / Alamy; 31 © Allstar Picture Library / Alamy; 36 © Advance Images / Alamy; 39 © Moviestore collection Ltd / Alamy; 43 © INTERFOTO / Alamy; 45 © Allstar Picture Library / Alamy; 49 © AF archive / Alamy; 56 © Allstar Picture Library / Alamy; 57 © Pictorial Press Ltd / Alamy; 63 © Alamy / Alamy; 68 © Photos 12 / Alamy; 69 © AF archive / Alamy; 71 © AF archive / Alamy; 73 T © AF archive / Alamy; 77 © Photos 12 / Alamy; 83 © Moviestore collection Ltd / Alamy; 86 © Allstar Picture Library / Alamy; 89 © Jeff Morgan 02 / Alamy; 96 © Photos 12 / Alamy; 108 © Alamy / Alamy; 110 © Trinity Mirror / Mirrorpix / Alamy; 114 © AA World Travel Library / Alamy; 117 © Photos 12 / Alamy; 119 © Moviestore collection Ltd / Alamy; 130 © AF archive / Alamy; 131 © Pictorial Press Ltd / Alamy; 132 © Moviestore collection Ltd / Alamy; 133 © Photos 12 / Alamy; 134 © Moviestore collection Ltd / Alamy; 135 © Blaine Harrington III / Alamy; 137 © marc marnie / Alamy; 139 © AF archive / Alamy; 147 © Alamy / Alamy; 148 © Trinity Mirror / Mirrorpix / Alamy; 150 © AF archive / Alamy; 152 © AF archive / Alamy; 155 B © Chris Hellier / Alamy; 158 © AF archive / Alamy; 163 © AF archive / Alamy; 164 © Steve Skjold / Alamy; 169 © Photos 12 / Alamy; 170 © United Archives GmbH / Alamy; 175 © Photos 12 / Alamy; 176 © Pictorial Press Ltd / Alamy; 178 © Pictorial Press Ltd / Alamy; 182 © Radius Images / Alamy; 183 © AF archive / Alamy; 187 © Michael Dwyer / Alamy; 195 © Photos 12 / Alamy; 197 L © AF archive / Alamy; 200 © Pictorial Press Ltd / Alamy; 205 © f4foto / Alamy; 211 © Iain Masterton / Alamy; 213 © Aurora Photos / Alamy; 214 © First Light / Alamy; 217 © Lebrecht Music and Arts Photo Library / Alamy; 218 © Rob Bartee / Alamy; 219 © Richard Levine / Alamy; 223 © Adrian Sherratt / Alamy; 226 © Cyberstock / Alamy; 227 © Ian Shaw / Alamy; 235 © AF archive / Alamy; 242 © Pictorial Press Ltd / Alamy; 244 © pierre rochon / Alamy; 245 T-L © David Crausby / Alamy; 245 B-R © Philip Game / Alamy.

Corbis: 145 © Jeffery Allan Salter/CORBIS SABA.

Getty Images: 142 © WireImage.

istock: 16 © Vladimir Piskunov; 26 © Servifoto; 35 © MJ Photography; 44 © studiovancaspel; 46 © Rapid Eye Media; 54 © Mansi Ltd; 61 © digital planet design; 65 © track5; 74 © SensorSpot; 93 © LiammoganLiammogan; 94 © wmiami; 115 © Jani Bryson Studios, Inc.; 116 © cmcderm1; 123 © Crosseyedphoto; 124 © Vasko Miokovic Photography; 153 © Graffizone; 220 L © Architect; 222 © izusek; 225 © FOTOGRAFIA INC.; 230 © Haider.

Rex Features: 75 © Startraks Photo/Rex Features; 157 © Everett Collection/Rex Features; 236 © NBCUPHOTOBANK/Rex Features.

Shutterstock: 22 © Caruntu; 29 © bg_knight; 42 © sokolovsky; 73 B © Perov Stanislav; 78 © Dmitri Mihhailov; 84 T © Randy Miramontez; 84 B © YanLev; 109 © ChipPix; 128 T-R © ChipPix; 128 B-L © Andreas Gradin; 196 © StockLite; 203 © Kenneth Man; 204 © Yuri Arcurs; 207 © Kenneth Man; 210 © Paul Matthew Photography.

122 © Vincent van der Hoogen; 155 T © www.rallytorestoresanity.com; 162 © Ali Reza Farahnakian; 202 © Daniel Snyder / Wikipedia; 214 T-R, C-R, B-R © Mat Deaves; 232 T-R © Brian McKim; 232 B-L © Traci Skene; 239 © Joe Starr.

PICTURE CREDITS | 256